Jacob of Sarug's Homily on the Presentation of our Lord

TEXTS FROM CHRISTIAN LATE ANTIQUITY

15

General Editor
George A. Kiraz

The Metrical Homilies of Mar Jacob of Sarug

GENERAL EDITOR
SEBASTIAN P. BROCK

MANAGING EDITOR
GEORGE A. KIRAZ

FASCICLE 7

Jacob of Sarug's Homily on the Presentation of our Lord

TRANSLATED WITH INTRODUCTION BY
THOMAS KOLLAMPARAMPIL

GORGIAS PRESS
2008

First Gorgias Press Edition, 2008

Copyright © 2008 by Gorgias Press LLC

All rights reserved under International and Pan-American Copyright Conventions. No part of this publication may be reproduced, stored in a retrieval system or transmitted in any form or by any means, electronic, mechanical, photocopying, recording, scanning or otherwise without the prior written permission of Gorgias Press LLC.

Published in the United States of America by Gorgias Press LLC, New Jersey

ISBN 978-1-59333-936-4
ISSN 1935-6846

GORGIAS PRESS
180 Centennial Ave., Suite 3, Piscataway, NJ 08854 USA
www.gorgiaspress.com

Library of Congress Cataloging-in-Publication Data
Jacob, of Serug, 451-521.
  [Homily on the presentation of our Lord. English & Syriac]
  Jacob of Sarug's Homily on the presentation of our Lord / translated with introduction by Thomas Kollamparampil. -- 1st Gorgias Press ed.
     p. cm. -- (Texts from Christian late antiquity ; 15) (Metrical homilies of Mar Jacob of Sarug ; fasc. 7)
  English and Syriac.
  Includes bibliographical references and indexes.
  1. Candlemas--Sermons. 2. Sermons, Syriac. 3. Sermons, Syriac--Translations into English. I. Kollamparampil, Thomas. II. Title.
  BV50.C3J3313 2008
  252'.014--dc22
                                2008019966

The paper used in this publication meets the minimum requirements of the American National Standards.

Printed in the United States of America

This publication was made possible with a generous grant from

THE BARNABAS FUND

and

THE ATHANASIUS YESHU SAMUEL FUND

Table of Contents

Table of Contents v
List of Abbreviations vii
Introduction 1
   Outline 1
   Summary 3
Text and Translation 5
   Entreating Divine Assistance and the Admonition to Give Praise 6
   The Wonder and Paradox of Incarnation 6
   The Law-Giver and the Fulfilment of the Law 8
   Simeon, the Witness Par Excellence 10
   Simeon, a Sign on the Road of the One Who Comes 12
   The Lord at the Temple and the Spirit's Beckoning to Simeon 14
   The Supplication of Simeon to the Infant 16
   The Enigma of Simeon's Speech 18
   The Ritual Offering of the Lord of the Heights 20
   The Paradox of Simeon Carrying the Infant 26
   The Spiritual Perception of Simeon 26
   Mary's Discerning Questions 30
   Simeon's Reply to Mary's Questions 32
   Mary's Confirming Endorsements 36
   Simeon's Supplication to be an Advocate and a Witness among the
      Dead 40
   The Concluding Prayer 48
Bibliography of Works Cited 51
   (a) Ancient authors, editions and translations 51
   Aphrahat: 51
   Ephrem: 51
   Jacob: 51
   Narsai 52
   (b) Secondary literature 52

Index of Names and Themes 53
Index of Biblical References 54

LIST OF ABBREVIATIONS

Bedjan, I–VI   P. Bedjan, *Homiliae Selectae Mar-Jacobi Sarugensis*, I–V (Paris/Leipzig, 1905–1910; repr., with extra vol. VI, Piscataway NJ, 2006).
CSCO   Corpus Scriptorum Christianorum Orientalium.
Kollamparampil, Festal Homilies   T. Kollamparampil, *Jacob of Serugh, Select Festal Homilies* (Rome/Bangalore, 1997).
OCP   *Orientalia Christiana Periodica*.
PO   Patrologia Orientalis.
Rilliet, Turgame   F. Rilliet, *Jacques de Saroug, Six homélies festales en prose* (PO 43:4; 1986).
SdDN   Ephrem, *Sermo de Domino nostro*.
Vr.   Variant reading.

INTRODUCTION

> **INFORMATION ON THIS HOMILY**
> Homily Title: On the Presentation of our Lord in the Temple
> Source of Text: *Homilies of Mar Jacob of Sarug / Homiliae selectae Mar-Jacobi Sarugensis* edited by Paul Bedjan (Paris-Leipzig 1905, 2nd ed. Piscataway: Gorgias Press, 2006), vol. 5, pp. 447–466. [Homily 165]
> Lines: 392

OUTLINE

Jacob of Sarug begins this homily with a prayer to Christ, 'The Eldest of Air,' 'Fashioner of Babes,' 'The One,' 'The Wonder,' for the inner composition of the required word and the instruction as well as for diligence and love to sing praises without prying into the exalted Divinity (1–10). Wonder is the natural and primary response to the great mystery of Christ. He is at the same time God and man, clothed in flame and in a body from the daughter of David to come to manifestation. Though he is beyond time, he enters into the time of birth and death. He is the 'Ancient of Days' and 'The High Priest' offering himself in the holy temple (11–20).

The Son gives the law to Moses on Mount Sinai. Now Christ fulfils the order of the Law in his own person as he himself taught. He subjects himself to circumcision as he is fully human and brings the ritual offering, manifesting that he is no more a stranger to his people. According to the Law he presents the turtle doves, which he had created together with his Father, as a sign of his self-offering (21–32).

By a bond in life the old Simeon had the task to bear witness to the Son (cf. Luke 2:29). The aged one gave witness to the Elder who became a child at the end of the times. The governing of the Son was made manifest by the supplication of Simeon for his release. The old man was placed as a sign suspended on hope against death, for the True One, the Lord of all times, the Messiah, who can give rest to him (39–64). Christ, 'The Guide' of all came to untie his ship that was moored in the harbour of life. As Simeon

1

was clothed by the Spirit he was impelled to speak true matters. Enlightened by the Spirit and convinced of the progress of the divine economy Simeon requests the release from his bondage to take rest in the bosom of Sheol until the day of the resurrection (69–112).

The author himself puts a question directly to Simeon regarding how to understand the meaning of the supplication of Simeon. Through such direct questioning to Simeon Jacob brings out the fact that the story of the Child in swaddling clothes has another meaning and it needs a deeper understanding. The Son is from eternity and even the order of time had its beginning in him. Therefore, Simeon is justified and was bound to make supplication which he did without doubt (113–138).

The two young birds were brought as offering according to the Law. It made Simeon, the seer of spiritual realities, mention the fact to the receiver of all sacrifices that all sacrifices and libations were received from eternity by the Son together with his Begetter. Holiness is transmitted only by him and sanctification is given only through him to the Levites' offerings. Simeon knows that all the OT offerings starting with Abel, Noah, Melchizedek, Abraham, Jacob and the Levites, were addressed only to him (139–164). Hence Simeon tells, "Take from your own and it is fair for you to accept" (170). Christ takes from his own creation the two young birds, and offers them as his initial sign which then makes its consummation in his supreme sacrifice.

Wonder laid hold of Simeon when he saw the Son in his arms. It is a paradox and then difficult to understand how a lump of earth carries the Sea: the Flood carried on fingers of soil, and a straw carrying the Flame, the Coal of Fire laid on an aged piece of wood and the Whelp of the Lion is carried by an aged man. Simeon has become a Cherub of flesh (177–188).

Filled with the Spirit and perceiving the hidden aspects of the Son, Simeon saw the onward journey of the Son for righteousness. The Son has a fight with the one who humiliated Adam in order to pull down the fortifications that error had built up. Through the inner eye, the sufferings, blood and the death of the Son became apparent to Simeon. All those labours are wearying and as Simeon is old, he makes the petition for his release from the burden of life (189–220).

Mary's discerning questions regarding the discourse of Simeon are suggestive of what the author brings into focus regarding the mystery of the person of Christ. Simeon in his reply affirms the eternal existence of the Son, his role in the creation of the worlds and its ordering. Now he is revealed since he willed it. He is humble in view of imparting what is due to human nature. The bonds of the life of all beings are in his hands. Hence,

Simeon finds it proper to seek release from him. Mary finds a new strength in the conviction and words of Simeon and requests him to convince Joseph as well as all other unbelievers regarding the mystery of the Son. Mary finds concurrence between what the angel told her and what Simeon proclaimed. Mary earnestly requests him to begin on the road of the apostolate that leads the future generations to the Luminous One. Mary finds in Simeon the first apostle (223–316).

Simeon requests his own release in order to proclaim the good hope from the Son's revelation and redemption among the dead. All the past generations, prophets and kings who yearned for him, would rejoice in him. He would go to Adam, Eve and Abel to announce to them that Christ, the Messiah, has opened the door of life by his birth. Abel who depicted the mystery of Christ's suffering by his slaughter will hear of its accomplishment. Simeon would descend to Seth and all other generations of Adam and Noah. Thus he would descend to Abraham, Isaac, Jacob, Joseph, Moses, Samuel, David, Isaiah and other harps of prophecy to play on them the sweet songs of truths (325–388).

Finally the author supplicates Christ, who came to liberate all who were bound, for the release of all grievous knots of strife from the Church and to gladden all in the manner of Simeon with the good hope of his faithfulness.

Summary

Entreating Divine Assistance and the Admonition to Give Praise (1–12)
The Wonder and Paradox of Incarnation (13–20)
The Law-Giver and the Fulfilment of the Law (21–32)
Simeon, the Witness Par Excellence (33–54)
Simeon, a Sign on the Road of the One Who Comes (55–68)
The Lord at the Temple and the Spirit's Beckoning to Simeon (69–82)
The Supplication of Simeon to the Infant (83–112)
The Enigma of Simeon's Speech (113–138)
The Ritual Offering of the Lord of the Heights (139–176)
The Paradox of Simeon Carrying the Infant (177–188)
The Spiritual Perception of Simeon (189–222)
Mary's Discerning Questions (223–244)
Simeon's Reply to Mary's Questions (245–282)
Mary's Confirming Endorsements (283–328)
Simeon's Supplication to be an Advocate and a Witness among the Dead (329–388)
The Concluding Prayer (389–392)

Text and Translation

ENTREATING DIVINE ASSISTANCE AND THE ADMONITION TO GIVE PRAISE

O the Most Ancient of all, who became a new born babe in the blessed woman,
open to me my lips to sing praises at your birth.
O 'Fashioner of Babes'[1] whose love compelled him to become a new born babe,
fashion in me utterance that is full of the beauties of your wonders.[2]

5   O Son of the virgin who was not known (carnally) by any of the mortals,
instruct my tongue to be an advocate of your songs.
O the One, hidden from the watchers, who became man in the body with which He clothed himself,
grant me (grace) that I may diligently become a hired labourer of your story.
O Marvel who cannot be spoken of by human beings,
10 bestow on me your love that I may sing praises to you without prying into (you).[3]
O Church, praise with your beautiful songs
the 'Aged Child' who by His birth gave freedom to you.

THE WONDER AND PARADOX OF INCARNATION

It is a wonder to narrate, while being God, He became human
and the Lord of (all) times came to the time of birth.
15 The Flame-clothed One who clothed himself with a body from the daughter of David;
the One concealed in His sender, who came to become manifest in the body that He assumed;

---

[1] Cf. R. Murray, "Mary, the Second Eve," p. 375
[2] Vr., 'your hymns.'
[3] 'prying into' the divinity is blasphemy; cf. T. Jansma, *Narsai and Ephrem*, pp. 60–68.

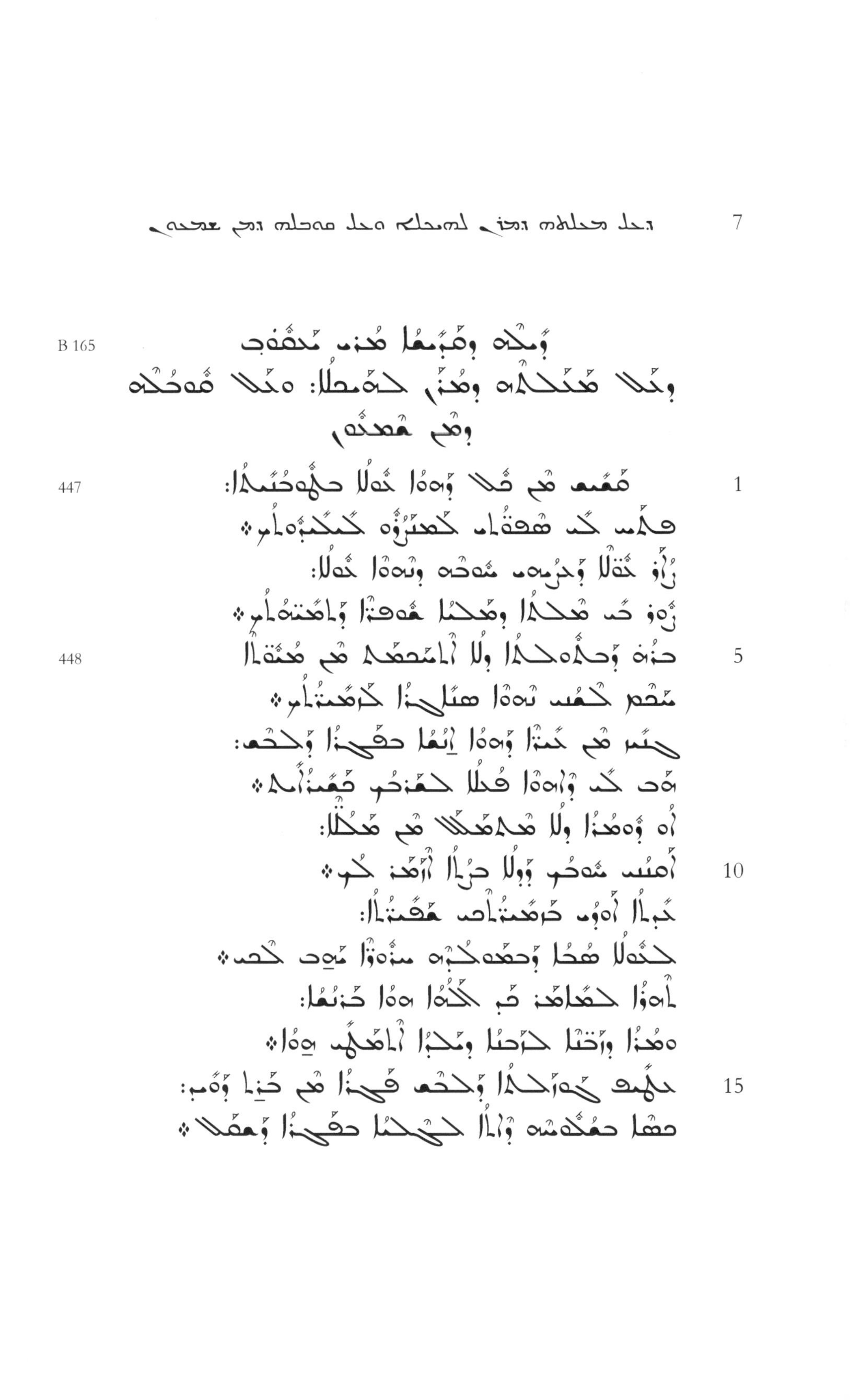

The Ancient of Days whom Mary wrapped in swaddling clothes Dan 7:9,13, 22; Mic 5:2[4]
and the aged Simeon held in his arms without his being weakened. Luke 2:28
The High Priest who gave atonement by the sons of Levi,
20 was being offered in the holy temple with the young doves.

THE LAW-GIVER AND THE FULFILMENT OF THE LAW

On behalf of the Lord of all sacrifices, who with His Sender accepts sacrifices, Luke 2:24; Lev 12:6–8
Joseph brought two young birds.
He gave the law to Moses on the Mount (Sinai) together with His Father Exod 31:18
and He came to fulfil in His own person the order that He himself taught. Luke 2:22,27[5]
25 He came to circumcision so that no one might deny His humanity. Luke 2:21
and He brought the offering so that He might show that He was not a stranger.[6]
Together with His sender he had commanded the waters and they caused winged creatures to swarm,

---

[4] 'Ancient of Days,' The application of the title to Christ, rather than to the Father, is probably due to the reading of the Old Greek of Daniel 7:13: "like (the Ancient of Days)", instead of "up to ...". This usage is not infrequent in Greek writers (and especially hymnography), and through translations of them it became familiar to Syriac authors from the fifth century onwards; see further, S. P. Brock, "The Ancient of Days: the Father or the Son"?, *The Harp* 22 (2007), pp. 121–130. Cf. Bedjan III, pp. 321–34, esp. p. 332 [ET, *The True Vine* 4 (1990), p. 46].

[5] Aphrahat, *Dem* II 6 (PS I 57).

[6] The Son has entered the world corporeally according to the Old Testament traditions.

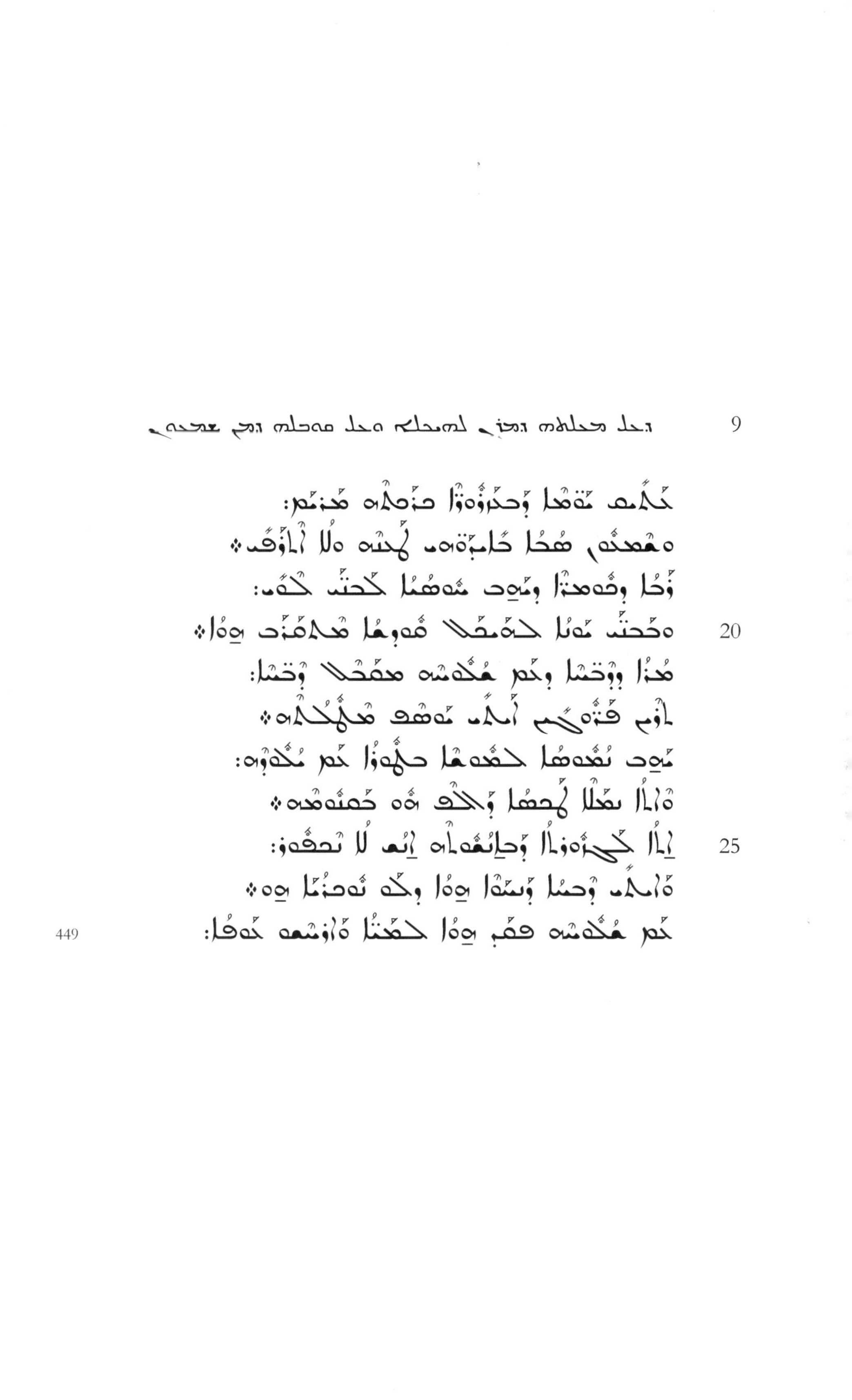

and by the turtle doves that He created, His own sign[7]   Luke 2:24
    was offered.
Mary carried the One who receives all, together with
    His offering,
30 so that according to the Law He should bring the of-   Lev 12:2–8
    fering to the holy temple.
Joseph carried the young birds which he brought on
    account of the child
and he went up to the sanctuary to offer according to
    the Law.

SIMEON, THE WITNESS PAR EXCELLENCE

The Spirit had seen that mediator of the divinity
and called the aged Simeon to give witness concerning   Luke 2:27
    the infant.
35 For the witness who came was upright and (he) was
    accepted
and for long years of his (life) he was giving witness to
    His truthfulness.
And therefore He was left behind in life for a long
    time[8]
in order to see with wonder the Lord, the Messiah,
    who comes in the body.
It was right too that one ancient in days should bear
    witness concerning
40 that Elder who became a Child at the end of the
    times.
He lengthened and prolonged for him the life by ex-
    tending the measure of his years,
so that with his testimony he should proclaim his faith
    that He is the Son.
Death was altogether forbidden to approach him,

---

[7] *remzā* is the divine thinking, pronounced in the form of commandment and realized by its own power. In other words it is God himself in action. Hence *remzā* is divine thought, word and power as in a single effect. Cf. K. Alwan, "*Le 'remzô*,'" pp. 91–106, (esp. p. 105).

[8] Cf. J. F. Coakley, "The Old Man Simeon (Luke 2:25) in Syriac Tradition," *OCP* 47 (1981) pp. 189–212.

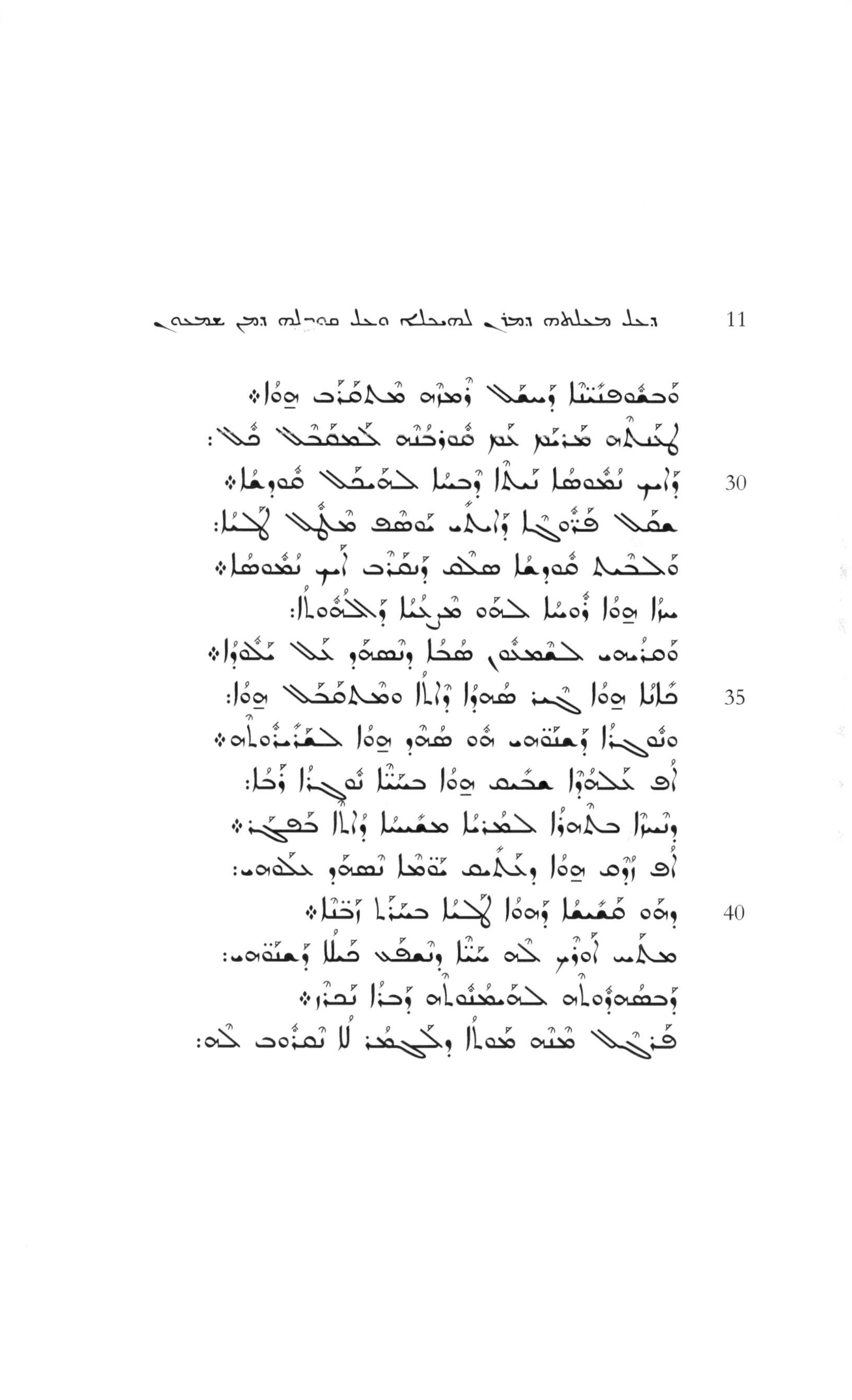

so that due to that reason the governing of the Son might be made manifest.
45 His bond in life was prolonged for a long life and he was allowed to stay,
so that when he made supplication to the Son to release him, the world should perceive.[9]
Generations have passed away but the aged one stays in prolonged life
in order to be a witness to the Lord of times in his prolonged life.
Generations fell asleep while the vigilant Simeon still waited
50 for the One prior to the generations who came to carnal birth.
The old man sat by the road of the world and gazed out to see   Luke 2:26
when the Lord of the world would come as He promised.
Death passes by on either side, but it does not touch him,
again causing many generations to pass on ahead of him, without ever approaching him.

SIMEON, A SIGN ON THE ROAD OF THE ONE WHO COMES

55 Simeon was a stone placed on the road of the One who comes
and He who rolls it away from among the living, is the Vivifier of the dead.
A great knot was tied among the living in a divine fashion
so that whosoever comes and is able to untie it would be truly God.
Although there were many anointed ones and priests, Simeon stayed on
60 to distinguish from them the True One who is his Lord.

---

[9] Cf. below, lines 291–318.

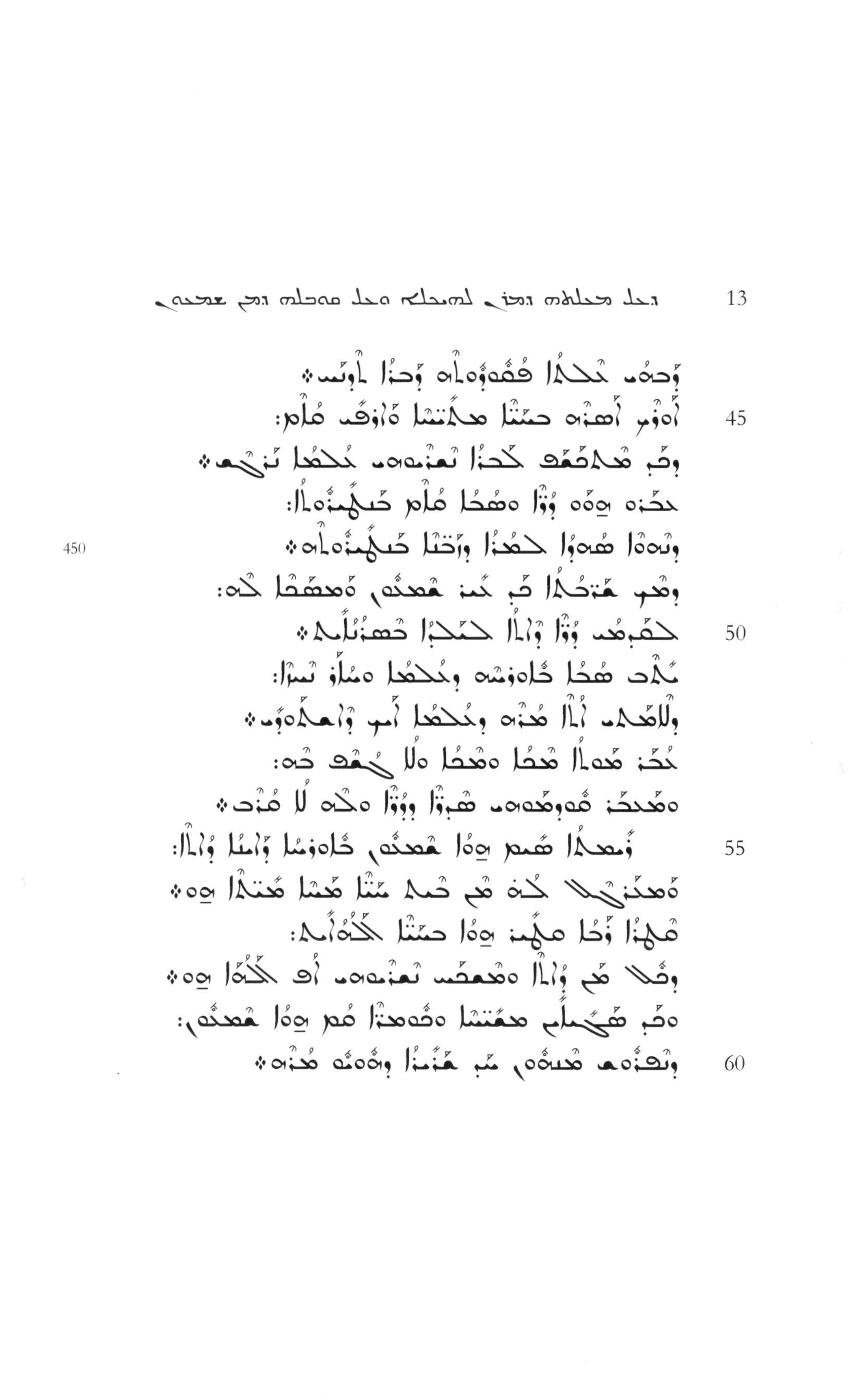

This sign was placed for that True One,
namely, that the one who would give him rest from
    his old age is the Lord of all times
He was bound in life and suspended on hope against   Gen 22:15–18
    death
for, once it was apparent who would release him, that
    One would be the Messiah.

65   The old man grew weary gazing on every babe (to see)
who is the one who would give him rest from the toil
    and the burden (of age).
And while this expectation was placed before his eyes   Luke 2:30
the time arrived for his old age to come to rest.

THE LORD AT THE TEMPLE AND THE SPIRIT'S BECKONING TO SIMEON

The Guide of all came to untie his ship in the face of
    death,
70   for it had been moored in the harbour of life until
    (that Guide) should come.
The young girl carried the Ancient of the generations
    who became a babe,
who came to renew what is old[10] by His birth.
He ascended, according to custom, to bring sacrifices,   Luke 2:23,24;
    as you have heard   Exod 13:2,12
and the Spirit called out to the aged Simeon, "Come
    and receive Him!
75   The Lord who loosens the bonds has arrived, come,
    seek from Him,
because He will release you as he promised, for He
    has the authority.
Rise up, O aged one, receive consummation from the
    Giver.
Behold, O labourer of the sacrifices,[11] the High Priest
    has come to give you rest."
By the Spirit with which he was clothed Simeon was
    moved towards the Child

---

[10] 'What is old' refers to 'the ancient things' (= of the old dispensation).
[11] Refers to Simeon, the priest, cf. *SdDN* 50,51.

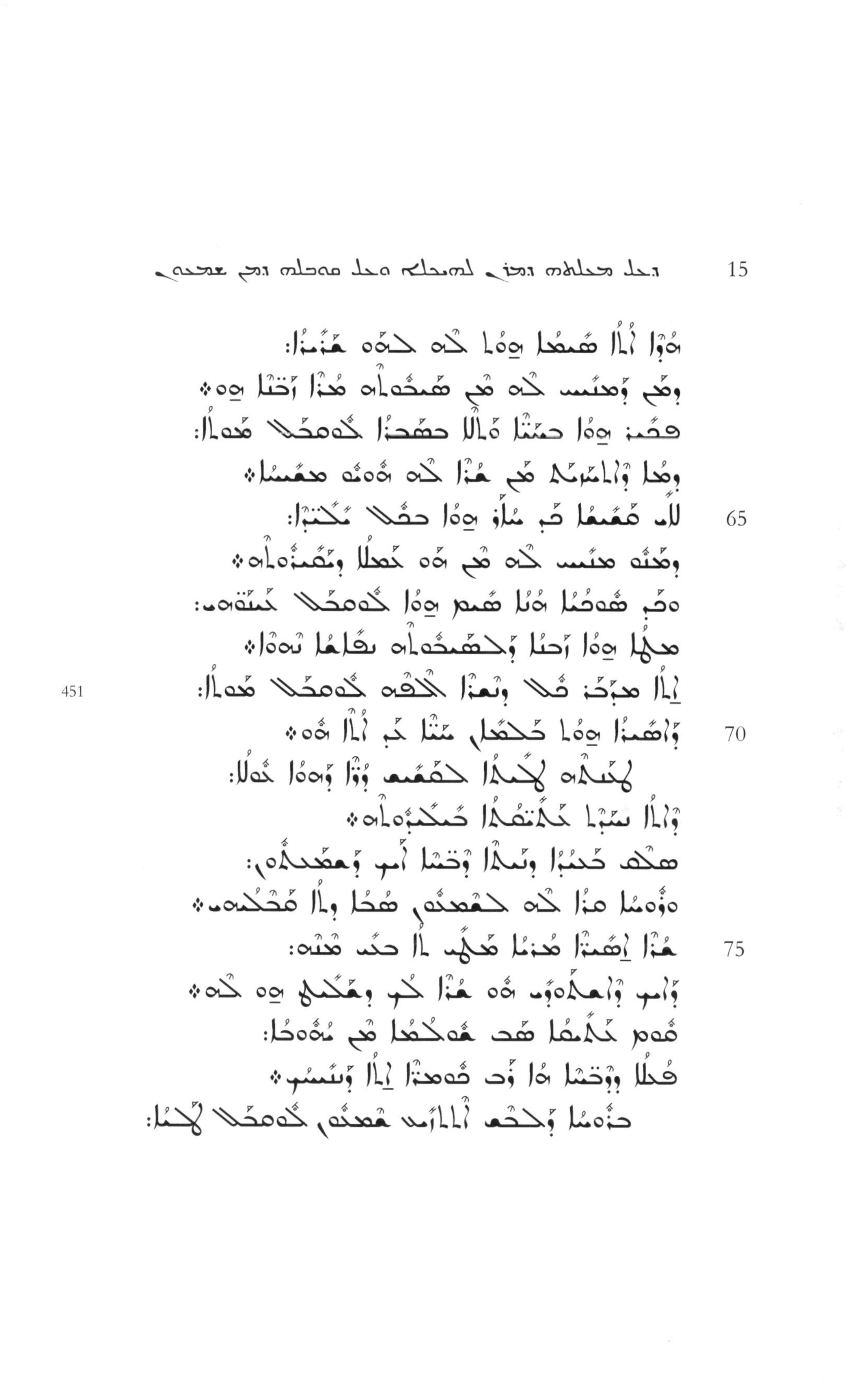

On the Presentation of Our Lord

80 and the truth compelled him to speak true matters.
He had seen the virgin who carried Him and he folded his hands.
With trembling he adored and received Him affectionately from her.

The Supplication of Simeon to the Infant

He began to supplicate Him, "Release me henceforth, for I have seen you, my Lord.
Behold, I have received you; henceforth, let me go towards consummation.

85 Behold, my eyes have seen your great mercy as you promised.   Luke 2:29,30
Set me free and let me be at rest on the earth until the resurrection.
I was looking for you to let loose my bondage by your birth,
grant consummation to the burden (of my age) that I beseech you.
There had been an agreement between you and your Father and the Holy Spirit

90 that death should not come upon me until I should see you   Luke 2:26
Behold, the agreement which came about in a mysterious manner is consummated.
Now, command death to grant me rest according to your promise.
Until now you have confined me here in the world, so that I might see you;
release me to go out now because I have become worthy to see your birth.

95 Behold, your gesture gave me the sentence a long ago,
that I should be bound until you have come in the body.
Behold, the sentence itself has been completed; release the bound-one;
because I have seen you, now is the time for me to take rest: it is for this that I have waited.
Let the wind of death henceforth blow upon my limbs

100 that I may go and reach the haven of rest, so that I may wait for you.

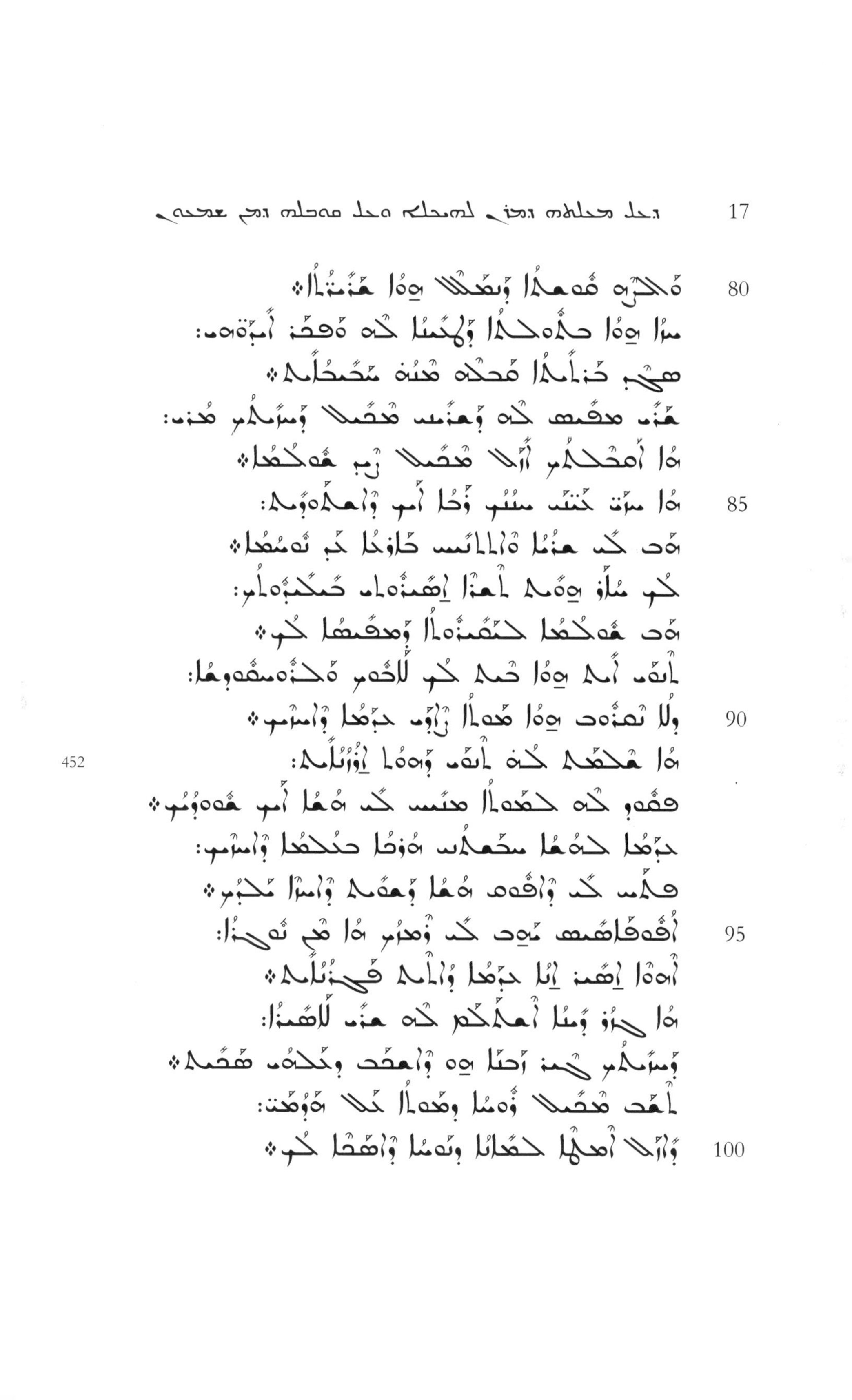

As One who commands all, sprinkle death upon my
  burden (of old age),
and set me free, the aged one, to descend to dwell in
  the bosom of Sheol.
Send me, and set me in the deposit among the dead
until you come and take me on the day of resurrection.

105 Command the soil[12] to take a little rest upon the
  grains of its dust
and with many you shall rouse it at the end of the
  time.
I have watched very much on the highway of the
  world to wait for you,
allow me to sleep and at the resurrection you may call
  me.
Sow me in Sheol with many who are scattered in it
110 and when the winter of the world has abated, command me to spring up.
Place me beneath in the furrow of the earth and close
  the door
and when you pour forth the rain of the (latter) end, I
  shall sprout by it."

THE ENIGMA OF SIMEON'S SPEECH

"O Aged Simeon, what is it you say about the child?
For these are words with which one might talk to
  some one aged.
115 Behold, you make supplication to the infant affectionately.
You are old and advanced in age, and why then is
  this?
It is (but) forty days since the young girl Mary gave
  birth to Him
and how is it that He hears what you are saying in His
  infant state?
Or is that word of yours not to be understood, as you
  say?

---

[12] 'Soil' here refers to the human person of Simeon.

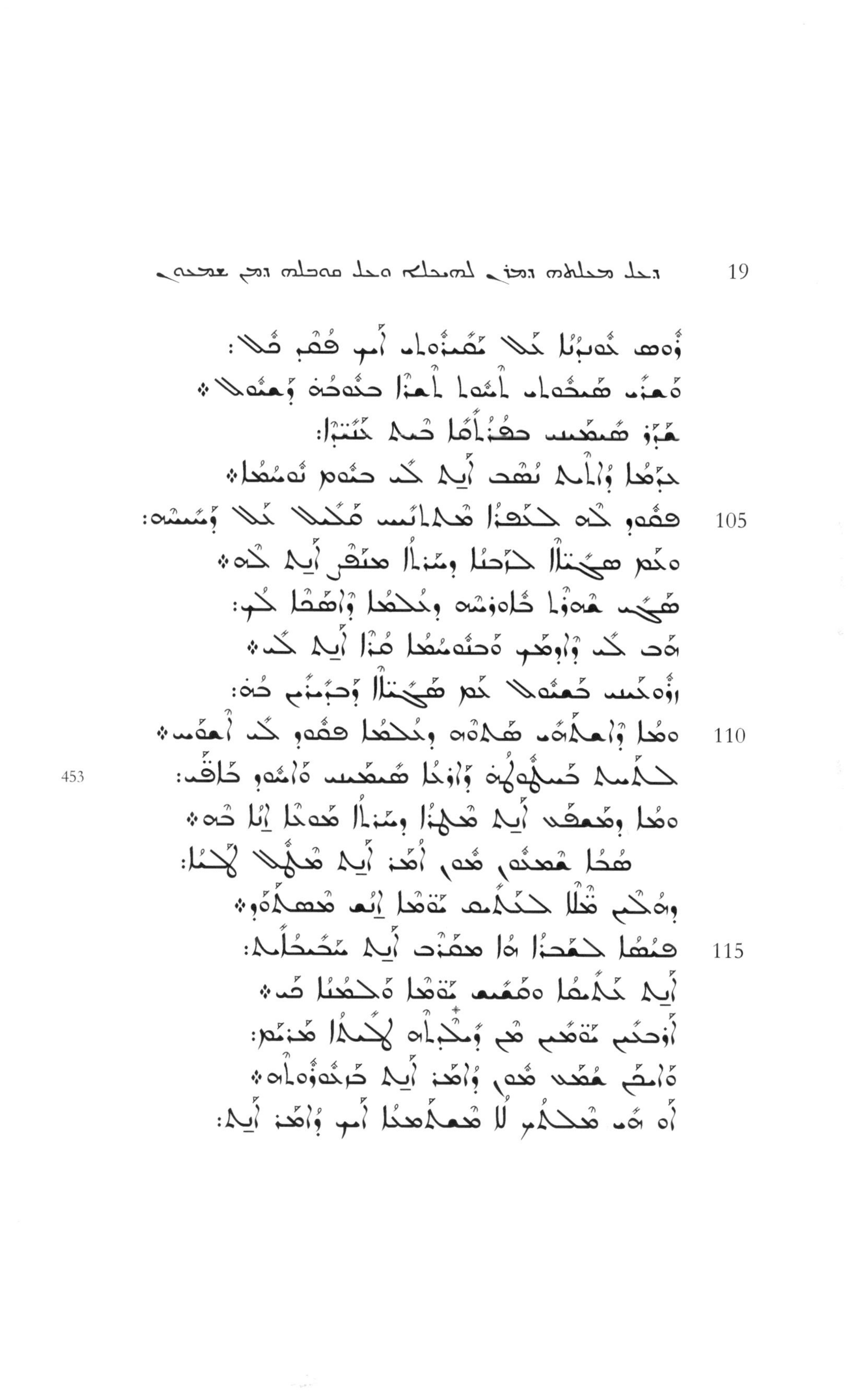

120	Or does the whole of your story seek another meaning?
	Or is your old age younger than that of the infant?
	Or is this child's age higher than that of yours?
	Or does His duration surpass your old age?
	Or has time itself taken its beginning from Him?
125	Why do you say to the (child) of swaddling clothes, 'Release me from the world'?
	Is it revealed that He is the Lord of the world, as you are asking Him?"
	The supplication of the old man bears witness to the Son indeed,
	because in a mystical manner His name had existed before the sun.
	That supplication of the old man in the presence of the child
130	would reveal the story of the Son of God, how he is from eternity.

"Before Abraham came into being I am."   John 8:58

Therefore, it is proper that Simeon made supplication to the One who was (already) in existence.

Then to the One who was able to release him henceforth he was pleading, "Release me,"

and he did not doubt Him who was being carried in swaddling clothes.   Luke 2:29

135   He carries Him in his hands and believes in Him that He is upon the chariot.   Ezek 1

He is held in the hands as a child and Simeon seeks release from Him.

He is revealed in His humanity but he did not doubt His exaltedness.

He is carried by him in the palm of his hands yet he believed in Him that He is the Lord of the heights.

THE RITUAL OFFERING OF THE LORD OF THE HEIGHTS

He saw the young birds that were brought for the sacrifice according to the Law,   Luke 2:22–24; Lev 12:6–7

140   and the old man was moved to speak about the child.

أَوْ 120
أَوْ :
أَوْ
أَوْ :
أَوْ

Then such (words) as these were spoken by the aged one:

"To whom shall I offer the sacrifice that you, the Lord of the heights, have brought?

Sacrifices and libations ascend to you together with your Father

and how shall I receive a sacrifice from you and to whom shall I offer?[13]

145 For the Father does not receive anything without you.

Behold, from eternity, it is through you that He accepts all offerings.[14]

Holiness is conferred upon the priests and to their sacrifices by you,

and it is through you the priests of sacrifices receive their hallowings.[15]

You are the one who sanctifies the sacrificial offerings together with your Begetter.

150 It is through you that the Levites' offerings are sanctified.

The perfect sacrifices were offered to you because you are from eternity,

and your Father granted propitiation to the ancient sacrifices through you.

It is to you Abel constructed the altar and offered his sacrifices.

In your name he brought the first-born ones of his flocks and their fallings.   Gen 4:4

155 The offering of virtuous Noah too was offered to you;   Gen 8:20

while you received it, the matter concerning you was hidden in your concealed Father.

---

[13] Ephrem, Prose homily 'On Our Lord' (cf. *SdDN* 48).

[14] Cf. Bedjan I, pp. 316, *9* – 317, *4* [Homily "On the Pharisee and the Publican," ET in *The True Vine* 9 (1991), p. 32 (lines 353–370)].

[15] Cf. *HNat* 25:16, Holy Simeon's priesthood; Ephrem's prose homily 'On Our Lord' (cf. *SdDN* 51–53) speaks of how Priesthood and Prophecy flew into Christ from Simeon.

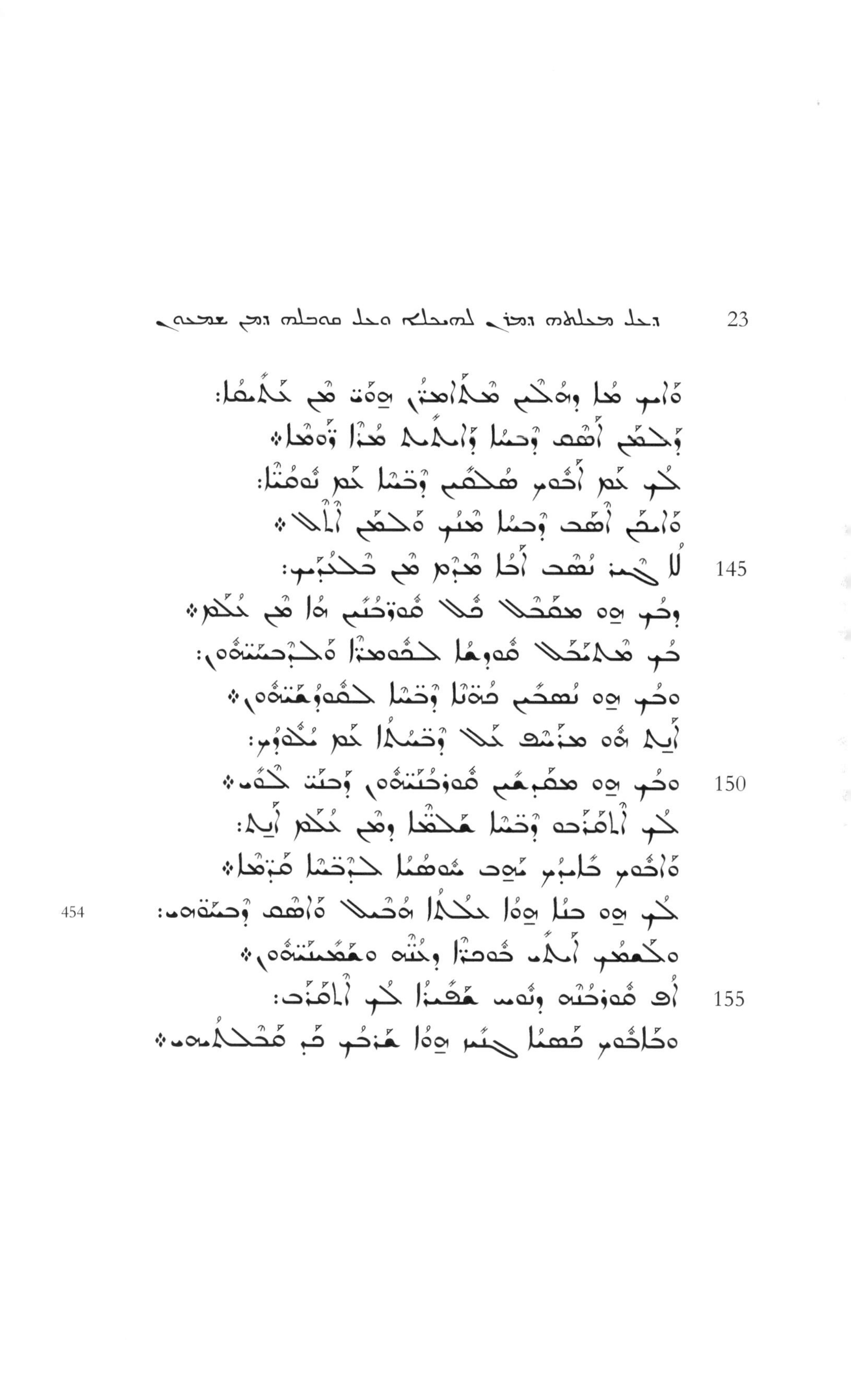

454

	Melchizedek[16] put on your great image with his offerings,	Gen 14:18–20
	and spiritually he had depicted your priesthood through his sacrifices.	
	Abraham built the altar at the top of the mountain for you,	
160	and your symbol redeemed the child, Isaac, from the knife.	Gen 22:10–12
	It was to you that Jacob had made the vow when he was fleeing	Gen 28:20–22
	and after you had assisted him he gave to you all his tithes.	
	Through your hand holiness descended to the Levites	
	and to you they brought all the produce of their tithes.	
165	There is no (time) when the Father is without you[17]	
	and He received all sacrifices through you and with you.	
	Then You are the recipient together with your Begetter, and therefore,	
	how shall I accept from you the ritual sacrifice which you offer?	
	If I receive it, I shall be giving (back) that same to you.	
170	Take from your own and it is appropriate for you to accept.	
	You have brought the sacrifice; come, receive it together with your Begetter.	
	Give me what you have brought and receive from me[18] what I am offering.	
	Your Father, on His own, does not receive sacrifices from anyone;	
	Behold, you are there with your Sender because He is with you.	

---

[16] There are two Homilies 'On Melchizedek': Bedjan II, pp. 197–209 [ET by J. Thekeparampil, Jacob of Sarug's Homily on Melkizedeq, *Harp* 6 (1993), pp. 53–64]; and Bedjan V, pp. 154–180, ET from Holy Transfiguration Monastery, *The True Vine* 2 (1989), pp. 30–55.

[17] Narsai, *PO* 40, pp. 68/69 (1. 498).

[18] Lit., 'my hands'

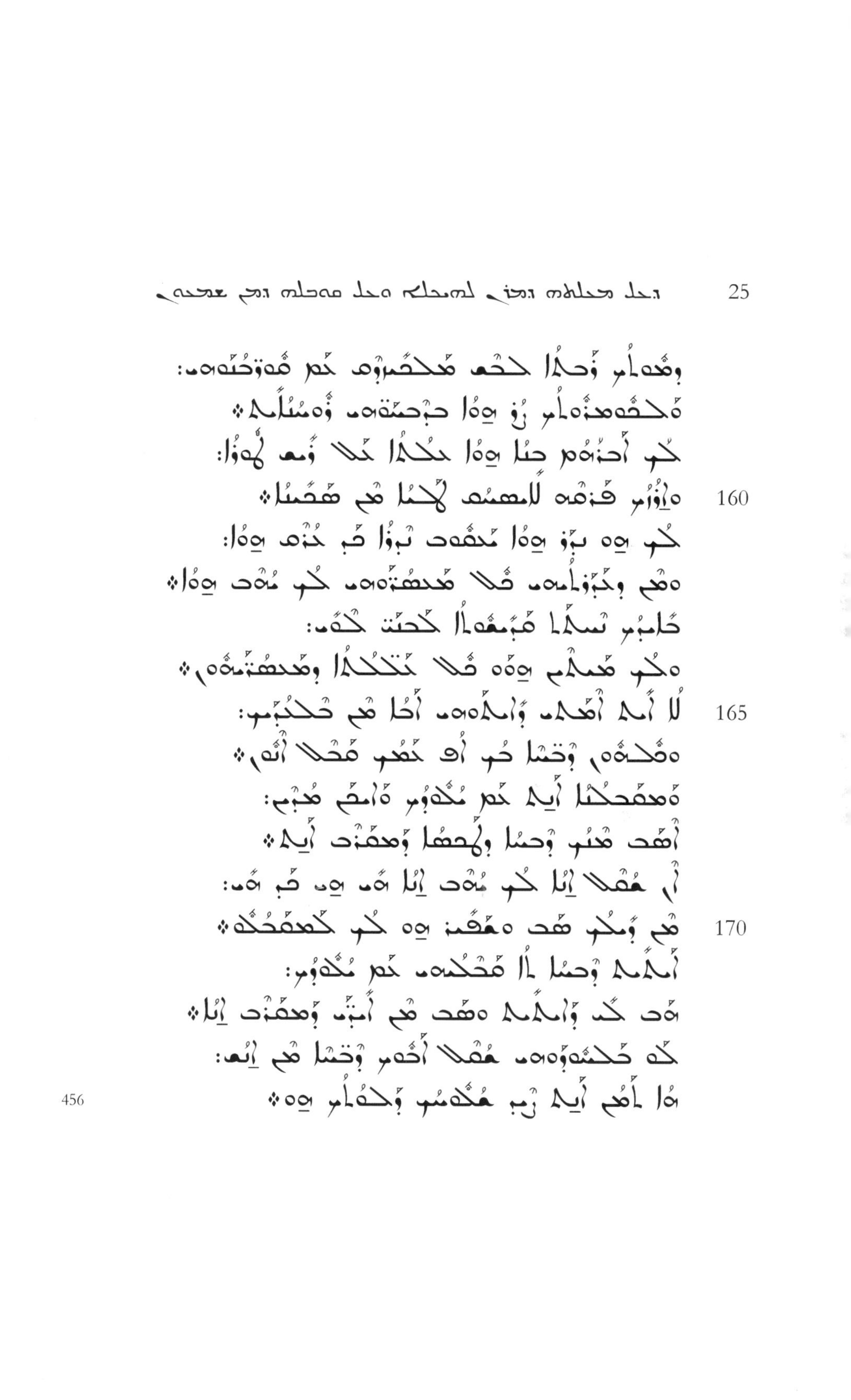

456

175	Behold, I am holding two young birds that Joseph brought.
	To whom should I offer if I do not offer through you to your Father?"

THE PARADOX OF SIMEON CARRYING THE INFANT

Wonder seized the aged Simeon as he saw the Son.
Then the righteous one was reduced to marvel on account of Him.
A lump of earth carried in its hands the Sea and it embraced it *[the Sea]*.
180 The Depth is collected in the cupped hands of dust but they were not dissolved.
The Flood is placed in the hands of the aged one, but it does not sweep them away,
on fingers of soil he carries the Lord of the seas.
A straw solemnly carries the Flame but it is not burned up.   Isa 6:6
The Coal of Fire is placed on wood that has aged, but it does not consume it
185 The aged one carries the Lion's Whelp and embraces it.   Gen 49:9
Yet, the might of that Powerful One does not terrify him.[19]
Simeon had become a Cherub of flesh on account of Jesus   Ezek 10:9–12
and instead of wheels[20] he carried Him solemnly in his hands.

THE SPIRITUAL PERCEPTION OF SIMEON

He was filled with the Spirit and was understanding hidden things,   Luke 2:26–35
190 and he was not ashamed to make petition to the Son affectionately:

---

[19] Ephrem speaks of Christ strengthening the hands of Simeon to carry the Strength that was bearing up all, cf. Homily "On our Lord" (*SdDN* 50).

[20] 'Wheels' refers to the chariot (cf. Ezek 1:15–28).

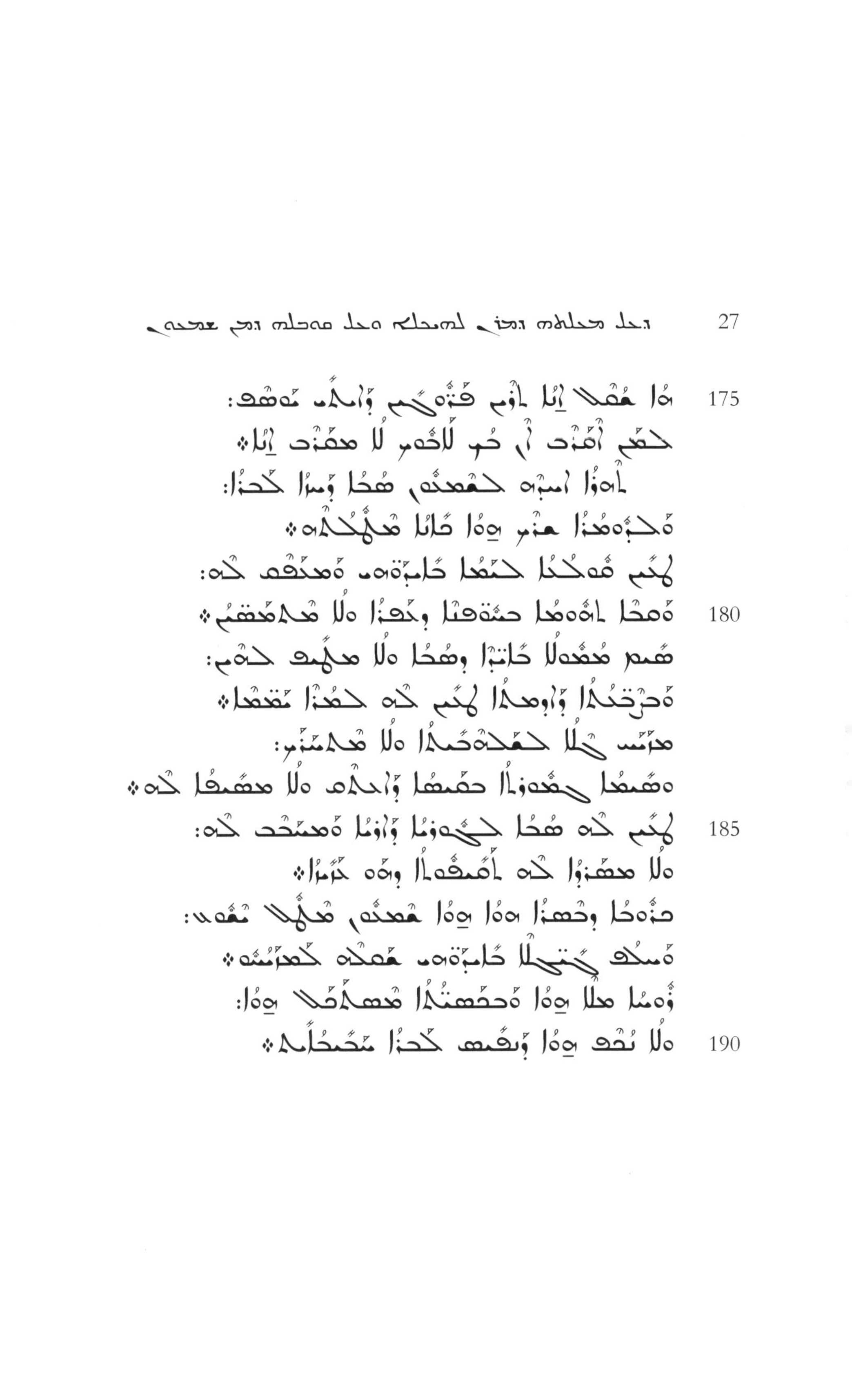

"Release me that I may go to (be at) rest a little among the dead,   Luke 2:29

because your way is wearying and I am too old for the journey.

You have to enter into a great battle on the way which you have set out on

and an aged man is not suitable for you to go with you.

195 You arouse dispute to raise up the side of righteousness,

and young men are suitable for the way of your proclamation.

You have a battle with the mighty one who humiliated Adam,

but I who am aged, am not able to take up arms.

You want to pull down the high fortifications that error has built up.

200 Look for young people, to go with you, because I am grown feeble.

You have the four regions to subjugate by your crucifixion,

and healthy feet are needed by you to run with you.

You have a new work to do on (throughout) the whole earth.

Have pity upon my old age, I am not capable of all your task.

205 You are devising (how) to build up the downfallen world;

But I am aged, I am too weak for your building work.

Your way is of slaughter and your face is set in the direction of death.

Let me go in peace; let my old age be not sprinkled with blood.

The path that you have set begets suffering to those who travel along it.

210 Give rest to me, and then you can pass on to your task.

You seek to be smitten by the captors in your bodily state.

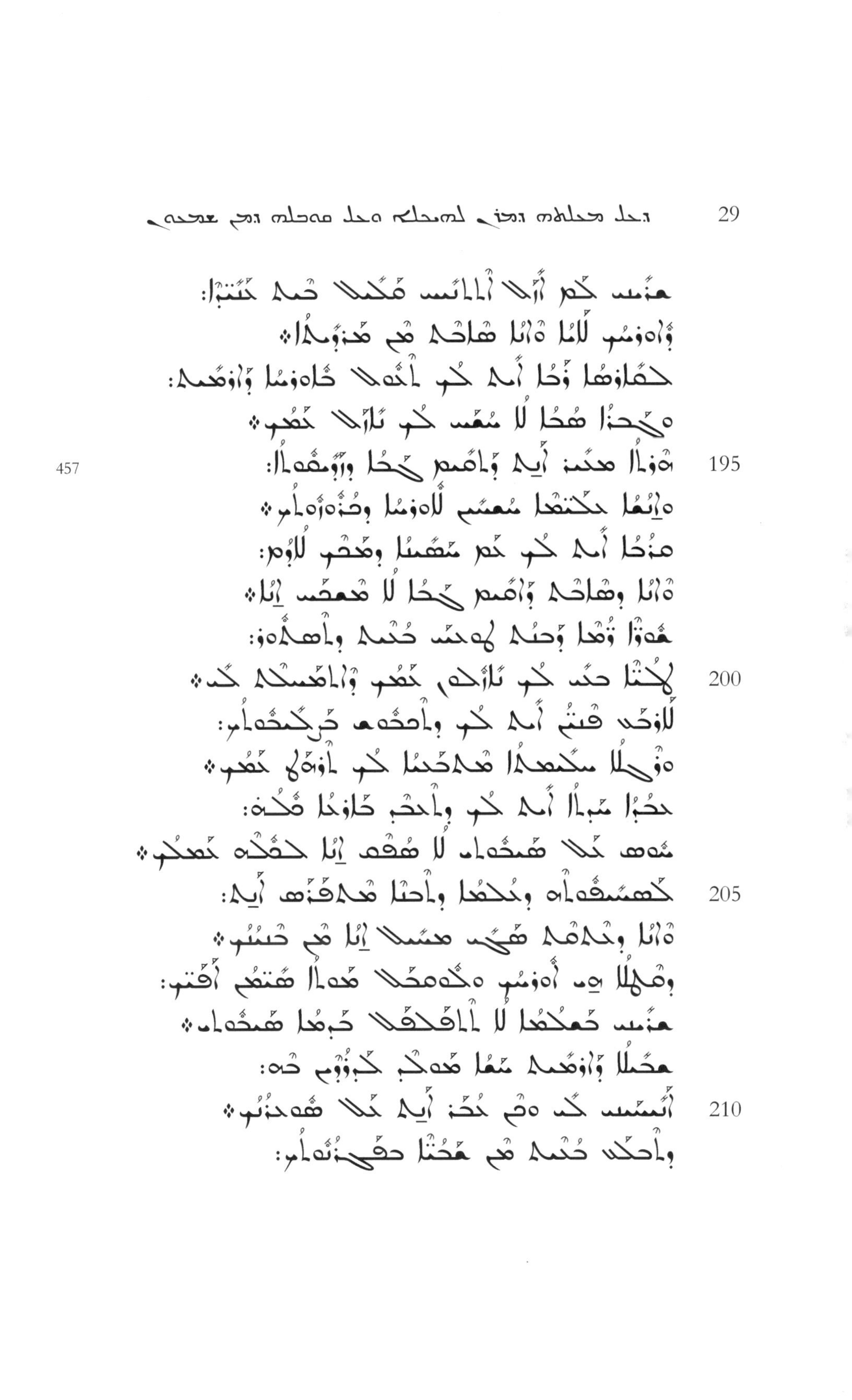

I shall take rest, for, my power to endure is weak.
You have the captivity of the peoples to turn away from stumbling-blocks.
Take[21] along with you valiant men, but I have become aged.

215 The whole road of your proclamation is sprinkled with blood
and because I have become old, I am not able to walk along it.
Your labour is lengthy and I am too weighed down by labour,
and because I make supplication, you shall not pass on without releasing me."
With this deep feeling, Simeon was entreating the Son to release him,

220 to be at rest on earth on account of the burden of his old age.
He takes hold of the Child and entreats Him without flinching.
He carries Him in his hands and makes supplication to Him as unto the Lord.

Mary's Discerning Questions

Mary marvelled discerningly at these things,
and with all kinds of thoughts she was contemplating in wonder.

225 And perhaps she had told Simeon discreetly,
"How will the child release you, old man, and when did he bind you?
Where was He seen by you, for you are old and He is an infant
and at what time did He make the agreement with you that He would speak to you?
Behold, since when did you have a secret privately with Him,

230 for, this story which you are speaking is like an old one?

---

[21] Lit., 'lead.'

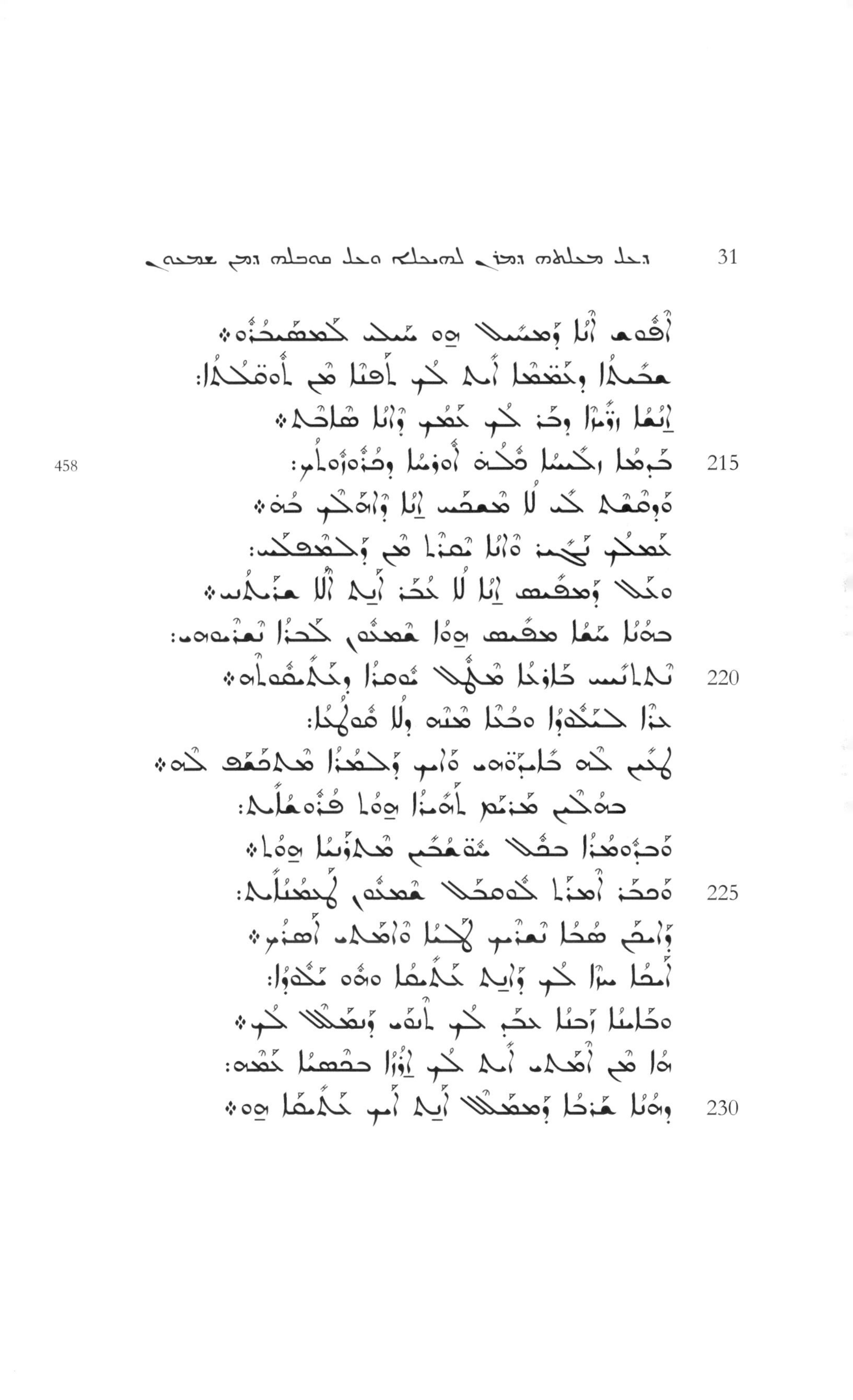

This discourse of yours seems to me not to be of this
   day,
because you speak to Him as though for a long time
   you had seen the Child.
Your story is hidden and behold, it seems to me that
   He is from eternity
but my son is an infant, and how does He know what
   you are saying?
235 On earth was he seen by you or in heaven? Disclose,
   and explain to me.
From the time I gave birth to Him He has not met
   you, except today.
I am not aware of this story which you tell
because I am a girl and you are old and advanced in
   age.
And if I myself am not aware of what you are saying
240 when and how does the child I brought forth know
   this?
How are you seeking release from Him and when did
   He bind you?
It seems that for a long time, as you say, you have
   been bound.
On which day did the small young child bind you
and how can He release you now, as you are pleading
   with Him?"

Simeon's Reply to Mary's Questions

245 Simeon says: "He is Almighty for eternity and it is
   easy for Him;
and He is more exalted than you; you shall learn from
   Him how He is.
"Eve, your mother, is immensely younger than He
for He is the one who governs all times and their ordering.[22]
Behold, by the hands of your Son the creation came
   into existence long before,

---

[22] Cf. Bedjan III, p. 322, *9–10*; p. 323, *3–12* [Homily "Why Our Lord Abode upon the Earth for Thirty Years," ET from Holy Transfiguration Monastery, *The True Vine* 4 (1990), pp. 38–39 (lines 17–18, 31–40)]; Ephrem, *HNat* 12:1; 19:10.

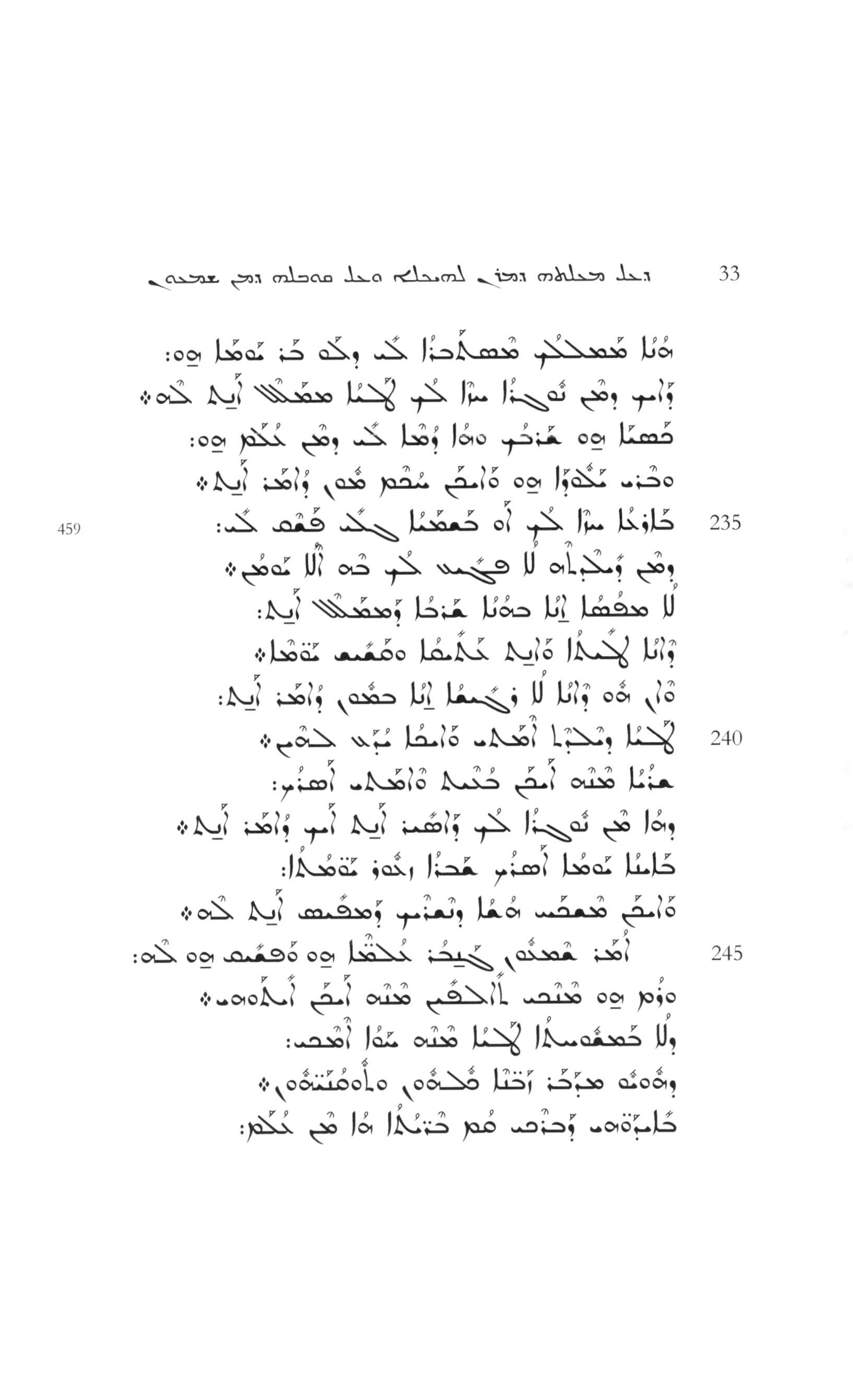

250   and He was with His Father when He was building the walls of the universe.²³
Through Him the world was generated to come into being from nothing.
The spacious womb of all extremities are contained in Him.
By Him was built the palace of (both) worlds from the beginning;
the house of all races was constructed from nothing by Him.
255   He, with his Father, set up the ranks of the heavenly hosts
and the legions of the sons of light obey Him.
The ardent ranks of Gabriel are commanded by Him.   Luke 1:19
and the fiery gatherings of the household of Michael obey Him.   Rev 12:7
It is He whom the Cherubs bless with trembling as they stand in awe,
260   then in truth His pure yoke is placed upon their neck.
Many thousands of heavenly beings are standing in His presence
and it is He whom myriads of the sons of the light bless.
Seraphs call out towards Him with the song, 'Holy, holy, holy,'
and before His brightness, 'Holy, holy, holy' issues from their mouth.   Isa 6:3
265   Three times they fill their mouth with hallowing
and then they call the Lord by His name with fear.
Here, He is revealed, because of the body He has taken from you,
for aforetime He is hidden because He is equal to His Father.
Here, He is humble in order to impart that which is due to His bodily state,

---

[23] Cf. Rilliet, *Turgome*, I.23; ET in Kollamparampil, *Festal Homilies*, p. 135; also line 130, above.

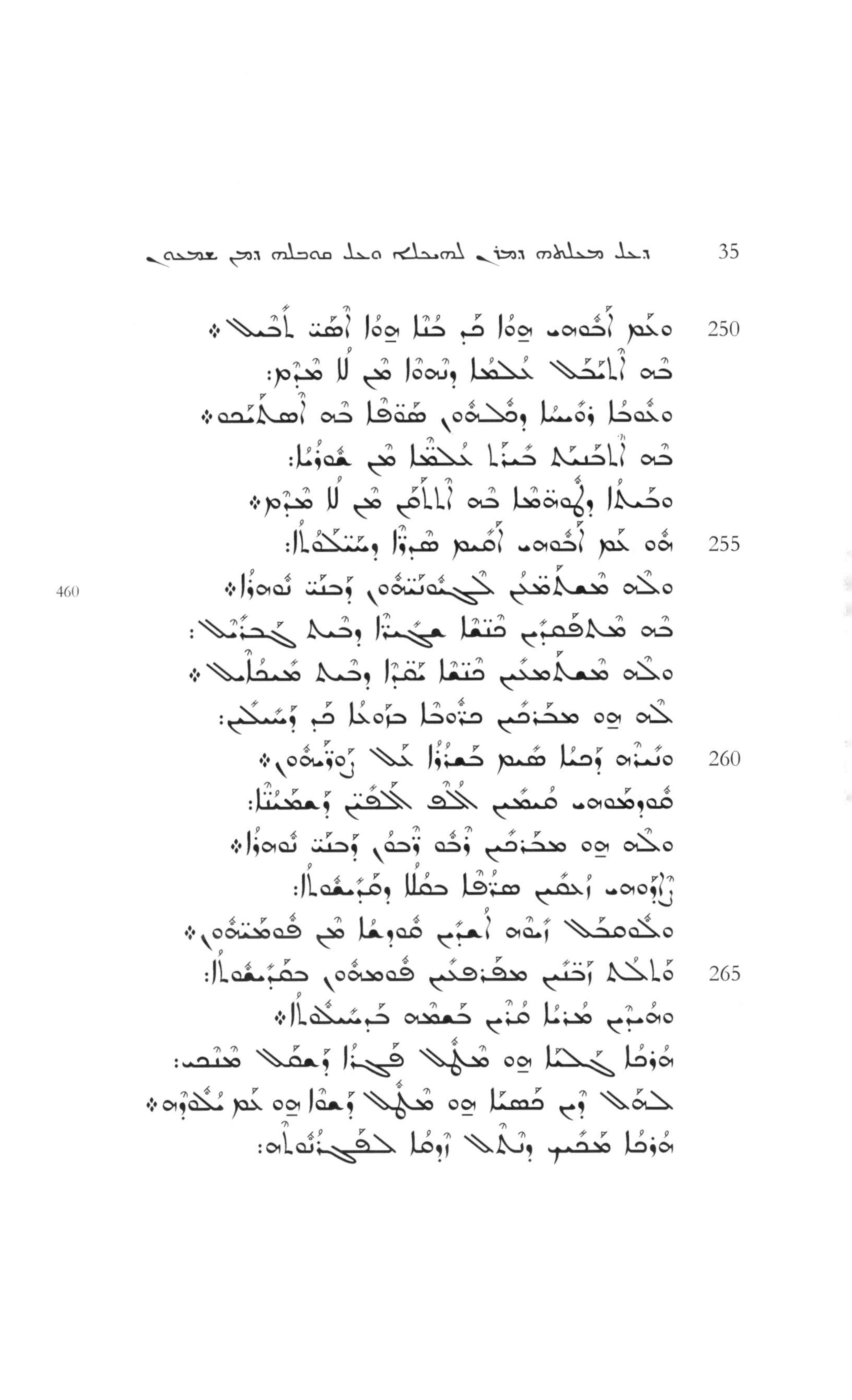

270 but above, He is mighty, to show the strength of His splendour.
Here we have seen Him because He was willing to become human.
In His distant place not even the Cherubs are able to see Him.
Greater is your Child than the creation, because He fashioned them
and if He wanted to show His strength, He would set the worlds on fire.
275 The fearful battalion of the Cherubs quiver at Him,
and the heavenly hosts trembled at Him when they were commanded
The gesture of His Father causes the angels to set off speedily,
and when they are sent out, impelled by Him the angels move.
He is the one who harnessed the seas with sand, together with His Father
280 and within the reservoir He confined the abyss lest it might flood to the earth.
In His hands are set the bonds of the life of all beings that are born
and, therefore, I pray that He release me, because it was He who bound me."

Mary's Confirming Endorsements

Mary speaks to the righteous Simeon: "Convince Joseph
for truly I am convinced of these (matters).
285 I learnt the whole of His story from an angel,
and as you are saying, I am understanding without doubt.
From the messenger who brought His good tidings I have heard them
and there is no reason to doubt about your supplication.
How is there room for a stumbling block to dwell in me
290 because, behold, I have given birth to a child, yet I am a virgin?

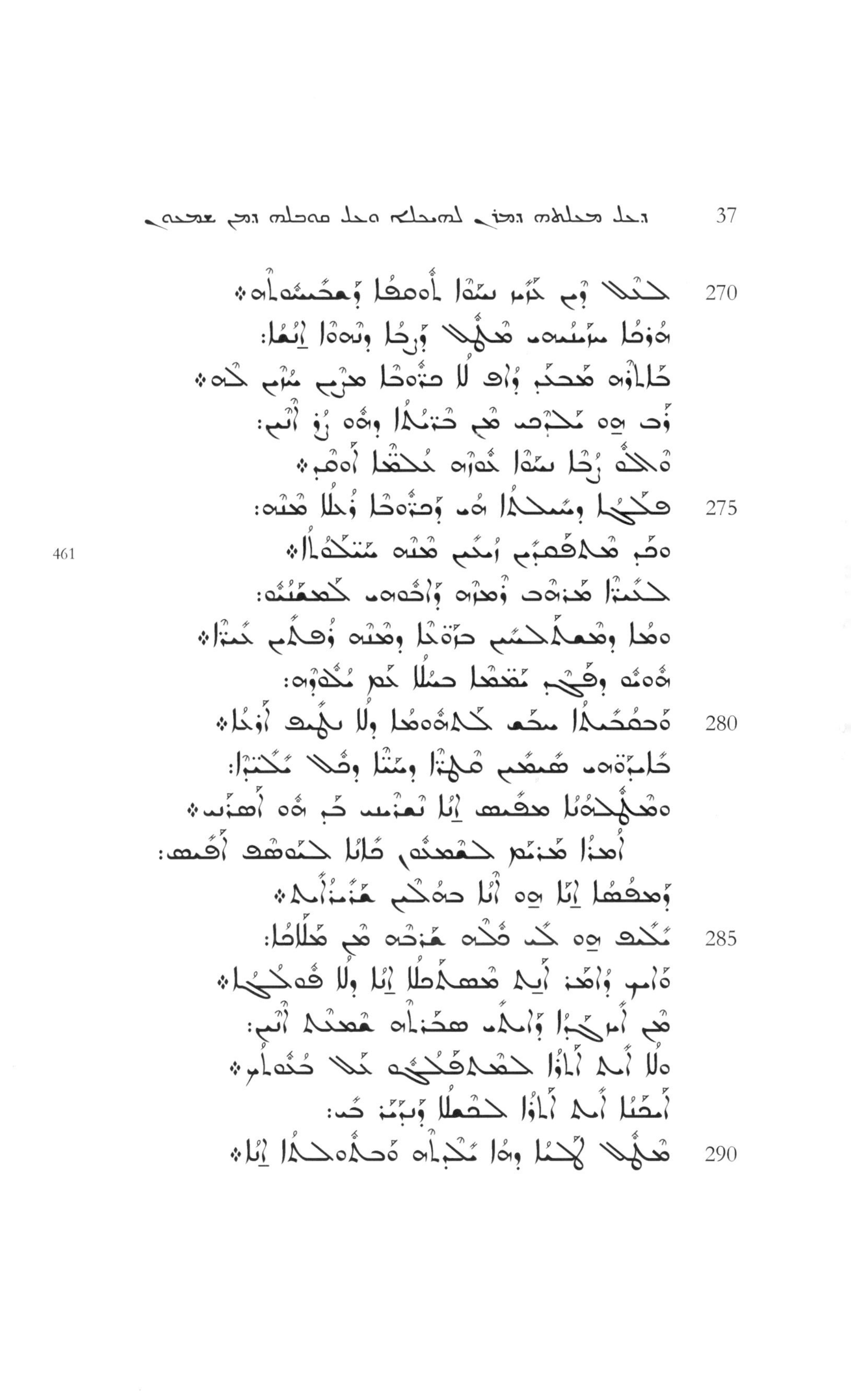

It is fair for you to be an advocate among the unbelievers.
Raise your voice, let all hear what you are saying.
Play your cither, O old man, and sing before He will release you[24]
and acknowledge that He has bound you so that the earth might perceive that He releases you.

295 Raise your voice, O aged one, as a trumpet
so that the world may learn that the Fruit which I have given birth to is the Lord of times.
O aged one, call out and give witness to the Son who is from eternity,
because I had been reckoned as an adulteress on account of Him.
Speak, Simeon, to the Jews and do not be afraid;
300 and reprove them, as how much they have accused me on account of your Lord.
Speak here at length, without ceasing,
so that the whole earth may receive proclamation from you.
Be moved and say everything in public about the child,
so that the universe shall perceive who He is and whose son I carry.
305 Be a herald among the unbelievers and reprove them,
because I am falsely accused at the hidden birth of the Son of God.
Seek from the child and give demonstration to the whole world,
so that anyone who is in need of requesting should make supplications to Him.
Begin on the road of apostolate clearly
310 and following your footsteps the generations shall go towards the Luminous One.
Gladden Joseph with the awesome things that you speak

---

[24] Cf. Bedjan, VI, p. 196/808; ET in Kollamparampil, *Festal Homilies*, p. 331.

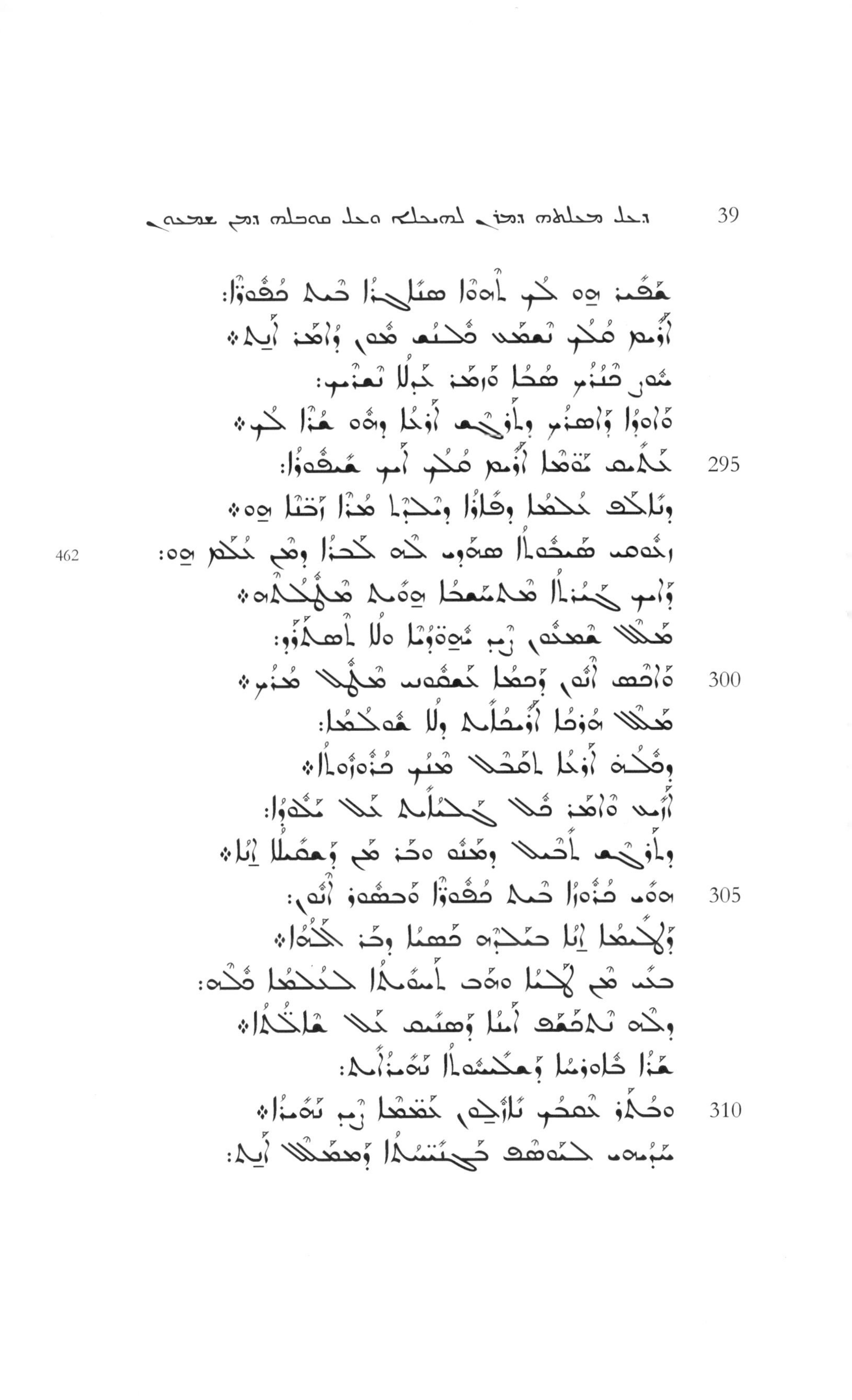

because he has endured much ignominy from the people on account of the child.
Make me confident with the utterance that you have imparted concerning the child
so that the false name of adulterous women should not touch me.
315 Stand by your power and lift up your voice in petition.
Also in your supplication give to the Adorable One what is His."
Because he was bound, Simeon urged the Son, "Release me,"
and Mary was hearing with amazement the voice which he raised.
She heard the story that called out that her Son was the Son of the Creator
320 and there came a pause to her false accusation on relief of Him.
It was delightful to the virgin ewe who was not (carnally) known
when the Lion's Whelp whom she carried was praised.
It was fitting for her, the persecuted dove, to give heed
when the Eagle, Christ, whom she embraced, was being lauded.
325 It was fair for Simeon, the aged one, that he was offering
supplication to the child discerningly, in the house of His Father.
It was also proper that the aged priest should bear witness to Him
that He is the High Priest who came to make atonement for the world through His blood.

Simeon's Supplication to be an Advocate and a Witness among the Dead

He was saying to Him: "Release me, henceforth, because I have seen you, my Lord,
330 so that I may rest in Sheol until you shall come in your splendour.
Release me from life that I may descend to proclaim among the dead

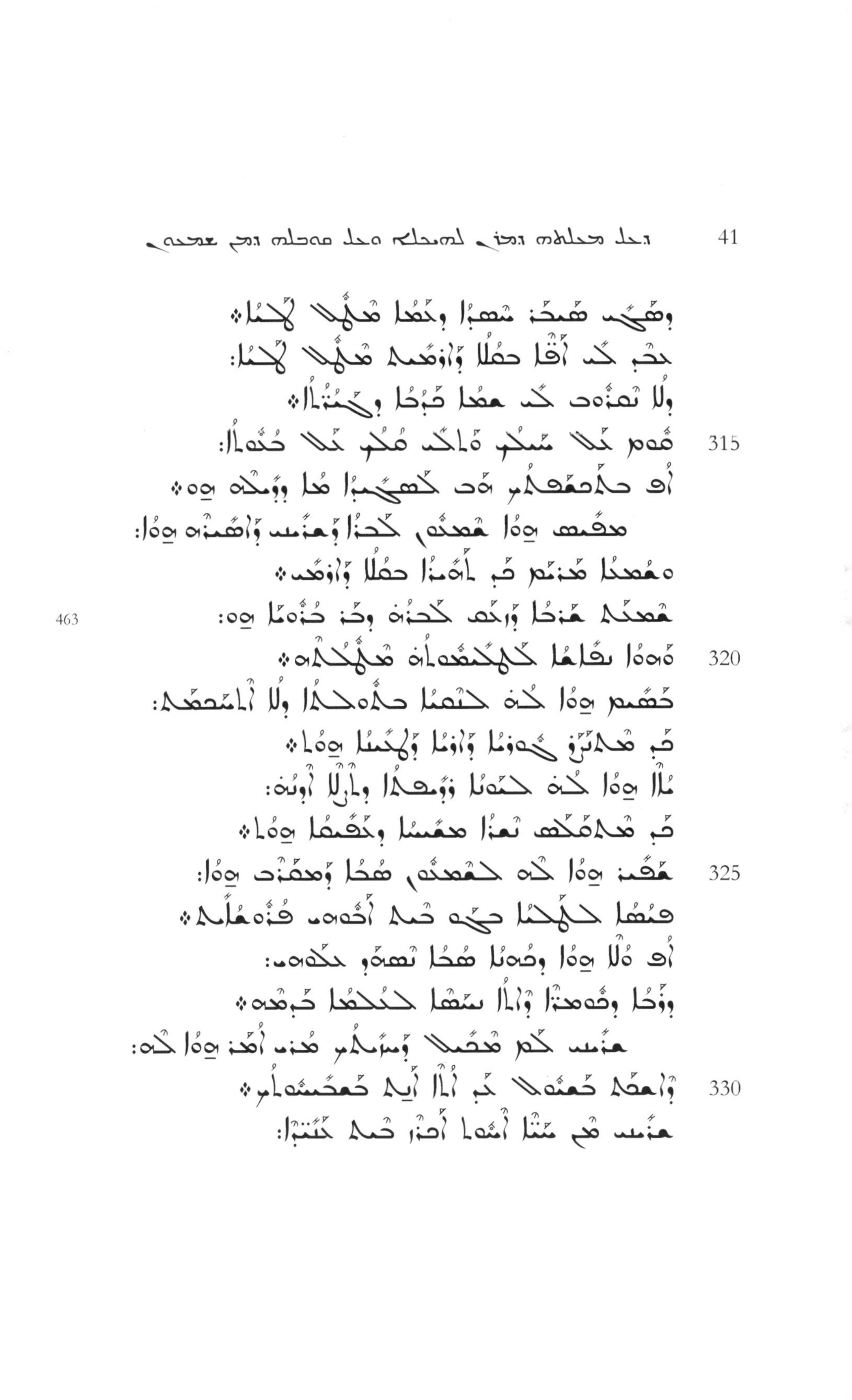

the good hope to the hopeless, from your revelation.[25]
Let me go before you and within the grave I shall proclaim your good news.
Then the early generations shall be preached to about your redemption by me.

335 It is good for me to become an advocate among the dead;
and if they become aware of by me, concerning your advent, I shall make them rejoice.
Towards the tomb is your road, release me to descend to it until you will come.
I shall cast commotion among the ranks of Sheol because the King has arrived.
If the dead become aware of me there I shall speak to them
340 about your advent from your Father and concerning your redemption.
Let me go to whisper to Adam in his ear upon the dust,
'Your Lord is coming to raise up the overthrown body of yours.'
There I shall narrate to Eve regarding your birth,
'Your daughter has given birth to an Aged Infant who will redeem you.'
345 I shall console her who was weeping for Abel;
When she hears from me about your birth that shall gladden her.
I shall say to Adam, Return to your inheritance,'
because Christ [Messiah] has opened the door of life[26] by His birth.
I shall declare to the expelled servants[27] regarding the return

---

[25] Cf. Rilliet, *Turgome*, I.7–8; ET in Kollamparampil, *Festal Homilies*, pp. 131–2; also Ephrem, *HNat* 1:52–60.

[26] Adam by his sin opened the door to death (cf. Rilliet, *Turgome*, III.32; ET in Kollamparampil, *Festal Homilies*, p. 242). But Christ by his birth opened the door to life.

[27] Through the expulsion of Adam and Eve, 'the Servants,' from Paradise (Gen 3:23) all offsprings of Adam too became 'Expelled Servants.'

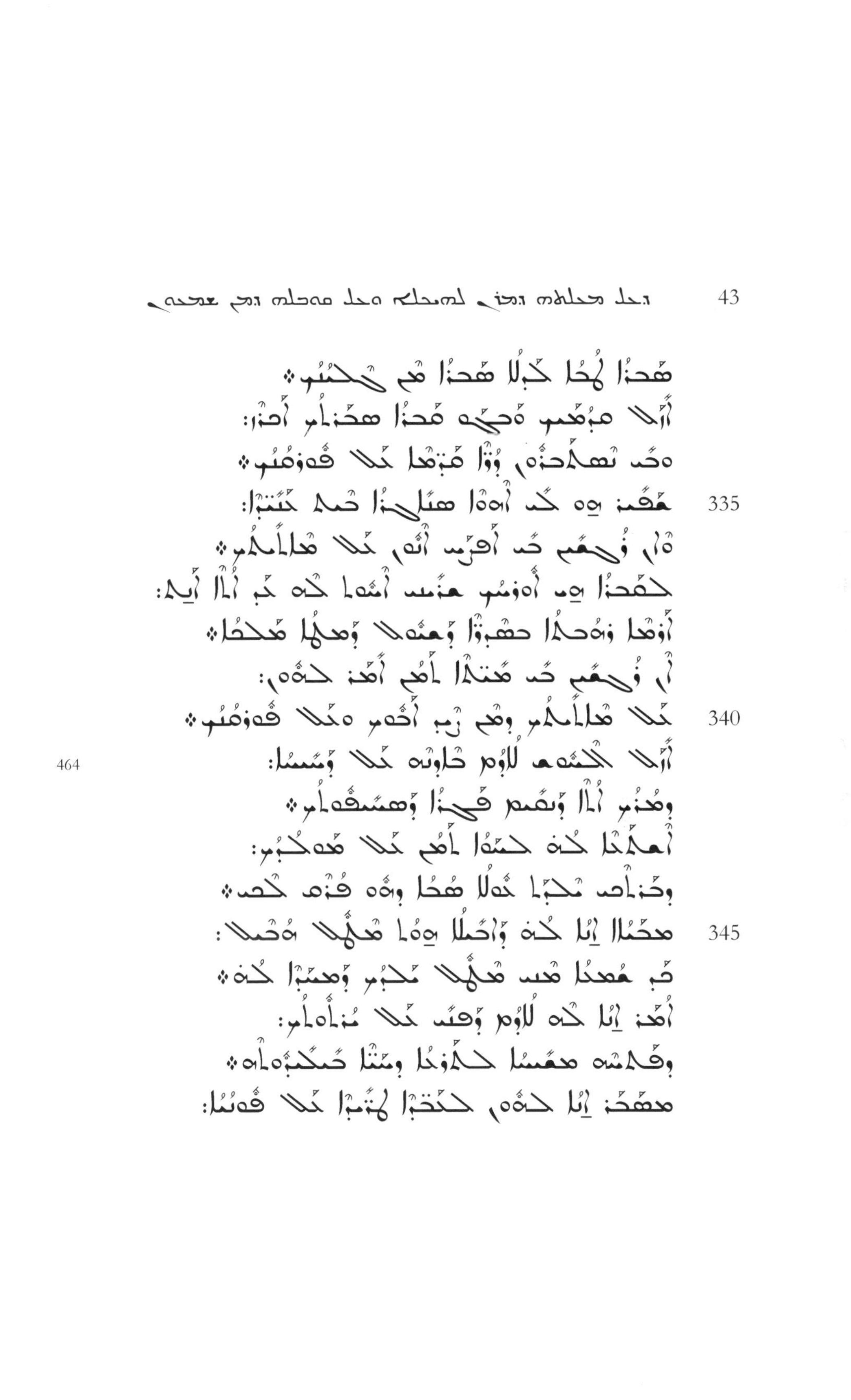

350 and with marvel I shall encourage them to give praise.   Heb 11:12,13
     Let me descend and sprinkle hope upon them with the tidings
     that death has fallen from its power and they are set free.
     Release me, my Lord, for from this time on, I have a journey concerning the good news
     so that I may carry the new tiding concerning you into Sheol.
355 Let me go and call out to the earlier generations who were cast down in it,
     'Be awake, give praise, because you are set free from the destruction.'
     Let me show the firstborn of the dead, the slaughtered Abel[28]
     that you too are travelling on the road of blood which he trod.
     Let me speak to him about the oppressed blood which will not call out again   Gen 4:10
360 because the image of the sufferings, which is the mystery of your slaughter, has itself been accomplished.
     Release me to the lower regions to see in the land the fair Seth   Gen 5:3
     and I shall narrate to him about your beauty which was concealed in him.
     Allow me to descend to the generations of Adam and Noah,
     and with your great name I shall lighten the dust from their eyes.
365 Let me go and be buried with Abraham who was eagerly waiting   John 8:56
     to see your day, and he saw your mystery, and I your birth.
     I shall proclaim to Isaac, the child who escaped from the knife,   Gen 22:9–14

---

[28] Gen 4:8. Four homilies of Jacob pertaining to Abel, Bedjan V, pp. 1–61 (Homilies Nos. 147–150).

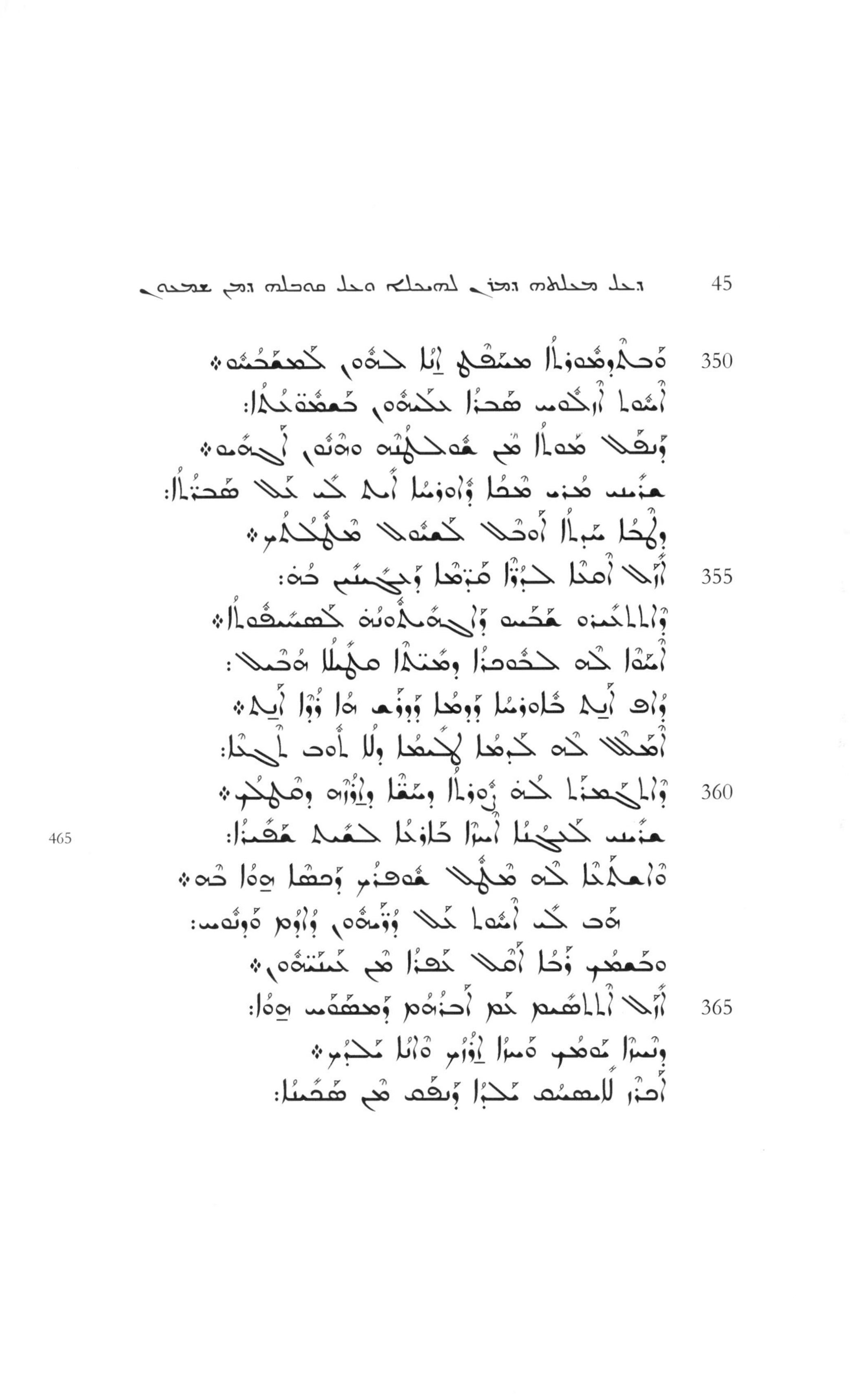

'I have carried that One, in whose symbol, your father bound you.'
I shall see Jacob, the younger one who became great because of your type. — Gen 25:29–33; 27:27–29

370 I shall also boast that I have carried you, escorting you in honour.
I shall narrate to Joseph who took care of provisions, — Gen 42:25; 45:21

how the Bread of Life has descended from the heaven for the whole world. — John 6:33ff, 50ff
Release me from here, that I may approach Moses and speak to him — Exod 7:10ff
that that One of whom he preached with wonders, was in my hands.

375 I shall go and see Joshua there, also Samuel
and I shall make them rejoice about your revelation, while they are sleeping.
I shall proclaim there in the ears of David as in good tidings:
The Shoot from your root has sprung up as it was sung (by him)'. — Isa 11:1,10; Rom 15:12
I shall uncover the dust from Isaiah and shall say to him,

380 'Behold, the virgin has given birth to Immanuel in a wonder'. — Isa 7:14; Matt 1:23
Let me pass over into Sheol to the harps of prophecy
and I shall play on them sweet songs of truths.
I shall visit them in their tombs, if I am able,
and I shall sprinkle them with the story of your birth, that they may rejoice in it.

385 The prophets and kings who were yearning for you shall marvel at me, — Luke 10:24; Matt 13:17
All of them calling me blessed because I became worthy to see you.
Release me because you have bound me; it is necessary that I should go, if you command it;
and though silent, I shall be your witness among the dead."

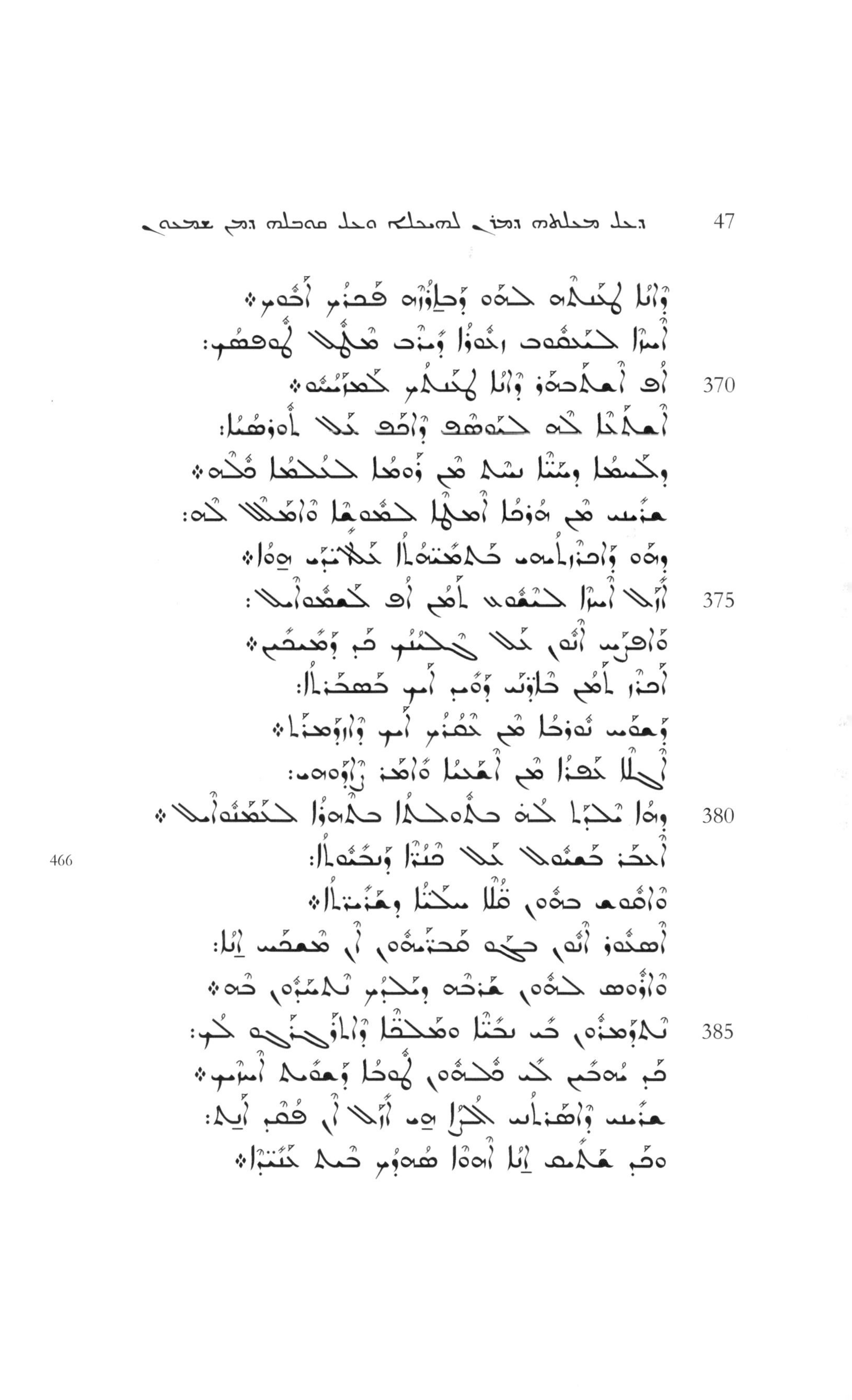

The Concluding Prayer

O Christ, who came and proclaimed liberation to those who were bound prisoners,
390 loosen from your Church the grievous knots of strife.[29]
O Son of God, who gladdened Simeon by His birth,
make us all rejoice in the good hope of faith in you.

The homily on the Presentation of Our Lord in the Temple and the Reception of Him by the aged Simeon is ended.

---

[29] A possible reference to the factions of theological controversies and social resentments of the times of Jacob.

ܡܫܝܚܐ ܕܐܬܐ ܘܫܪܐ ܡܪܝܐ ܠܒܪܢܫܐ ܗܘܐ:
ܗܢܘ ܡܢ ܥܒܕܬ ܩܛܪܐ ܥܣܩܐ ܕܒܪܢܫܘܬܐ؞
ܟܕ ܐܠܗܐ ܕܚܕ ܒܩܢܘܡܗ ܒܡܠܒܫܘܬܗ:
ܚܙܐ ܠܟܠܗ ܒܣܒܪܐ ܛܠܝܐ ܕܗܝܡܢܘܬܝ؞

ܫܠܡ ܡܐܡܪܐ ܕܥܠ ܡܥܠܬܗ ܕܡܪܢ ܠܗܝܟܠܐ:
ܘܩܘܒܠܗ ܕܡܢ ܫܡܥܘܢ ܣܒܐ.

BIBLIOGRAPHY OF WORKS CITED

(A) ANCIENT AUTHORS, EDITIONS AND TRANSLATIONS

Aphrahat:

J. Parisot, *Aphraatis Sapientis Persae Demonstrationes* (Patrologia Syriaca I.1–2; Paris, 1894, 1907).

K. Valavanolickal, *Aphrahat, Demonstrations* I–II (Moran 'Etho 23–4; Kottayam, 2005).

Ephrem:

E. Beck, *Des heiligen Ephraem des Syrers Hymnen de Nativitate (Epiphania)* (CSCO 186–7 = Scr. Syri 82–3; 1959).

_____, *Des heiligen Ephraem des Syrers Sermo de Domino nostro* (CSCO 270–1 = Scr. Syri 116–7; 1966).

Jacob:

P. Bedjan, *Homiliae Selectae Mar-Jacobi Sarugensis*, I–V (Paris/Leipzig, 1905–10; repr., with added Vol. VI, Piscataway, 2006).

Holy Transfiguration Monastery, "A Homily [on Melchizedek] by Mar Jacob of Serugh,", *The True Vine* 2 (1989), 30–55.

_____, "A Homily that explains why our Lord abode upon the Earth for thirty years before he wrought miracles in the world, by Mar Jacob, bishop of Serugh," *The True Vine* 4 (1990), 37–49.

_____, "A Homily on the Pharisee and the Publican, by Mar Jacob, bishop of Serugh, *The True Vine* 9 (1991), 19–34.

T. Kollamparampil, *Jacob of Serugh, Select Festal Homilies* (Rome/Bangalore, 1997).

F. Rilliet, *Jacques de Saroug, Six homélies festales en prose* (PO 43:4; 1986).

J. Thekeparampil, "Jacob of Sarug's Homily on Malkizedeq," *The Harp* 6 (1993), 53–64.

Narsai

F. McLeod, *Narsai's Metrical Homilies on the Nativity, Epiphany, Passion, Resurrection and Ascension* (PO 40:1; 1979).

(B) SECONDARY LITERATURE

K. Alwan, "Le *'remzo'* dans la pensée de Jacques de Saroug," *Parole de l'Orient* 15 (1988/9), 91–106.

S. P. Brock, "The Ancient of Days: the Father or the Son?," *The Harp* (forthcoming).

J. F. Coakley, "The Old Man Simeon in Syriac tradition," OCP 47 (1981), 189–212

T. Jansma, "Narsai and Ephrem," *Parole de l'Orient* 1 (1970), 60–66.

R. Murray, "Mary, the Second Eve in the early Syriac Fathers,' *Eastern Churches Review* 3 (1974), 372–84.

Index of Names and Themes

Abel, 153, 345, 357
Abraham, 131, 159, 365
Adam, 197, 341, 347, 363
beauty, 362
bondage, 87
captivity, 213
David, 15, 377
Eve, 247, 343
faith, 42, 391
Gabriel, 257
holiness, 163
hope, 63, 332, 351, 392
Immanuel, 380
Jacob, 161, 369
Joseph, 22, 31, 175, 283, 311, 371
Joshua, 375

liberation, 389
love, 3, 10
Mary, 17, 29, 117, 223, 282, 318
Melchizedek, 157
Michael, 258
Moses, 23, 373
Noah, 155, 363
redemption, 334, 340
righteousness, 195
Samuel, 375
Sheol, 103, 109, 330, 338, 354, 381
Simeon, 18, 34, 49, 55, 59, 74, 79, 113, 136, 177, 187, 219, 225, 245, 283, 299, 317, 325, 391
strength, 270, 274
suffering, 209, 360

INDEX OF BIBLICAL REFERENCES

Gen
    4:10   359
    4:4   154
    5:3   361
    8:20   155
    14:18–20   157
    22:9–14   367
    22:10–12   160
    22:15–18   63
    25:29–33   369
    27:27–29   369
    28:20–22   161
    42:25   371
    45:21   371
    49:9   185

Exod
    13:12   73
    13:2   73
    31:18   23
    7:10   373

Lev
    12:2–8   30
    12:6–7   139
    12:6–8   21

Isa
    6:3   264
    11:1   378
    11:10   378
    6:6   183
    7:14   380

Ezek
    1   135
    10:9–12   187

Dan
    7:13   17
    7:22   17
    7:9   17

Mic
    5:2   17

Matt
    1:23   380
    13:17   385

Luke
    1:19   257
    10:24   385
    2:21   25
    2:22   24
    2:22–24   139
    2:23   73
    2:24   21, 28
    2:26   51, 90
    2:26–35   189
    2:27   34
    2:28   18
    2:29   85, 134, 191
    2:30   67, 85

John
    6:33   372
    6:50   372
    8:56   365

8:58	131	Heb	
		11:12	350
Rom		11:13	350
15:12	379		
		Rev	
		12:7	258